Excel University.

Featuring Excel 2013 for Windows
Microsoft Excel® Training for CPAs
and Accounting Professionals

VOLUME 3

A walk-through of the Excel® features, functions, and techniques that improve the productivity of accountants.

During his live CPE training sessions, Jeff Lenning, CPA CITP, has shown thousands of CPAs and accounting professionals across the country how to use Excel more effectively and leverage its power to improve efficiency and reduce the time it takes to complete job tasks. This series of books is a comprehensive collection of the features, functions, and techniques that directly benefit accountants working in industry, public practice, consulting, and the nonprofit sector. Each book in the Excel University series includes narrative, screenshots, Excel practice files, and video content. This series uses a hands-on approach to learning and provides practice files and exercises that demonstrate the practical application of the items presented in each chapter.

JEFF LENNING, CPA CITP
CLICK CONSULTING, INC.

Excel University – Volume 3
By: Jeff Lenning, CPA CITP
Version: 2.0

ISBN-10: 1500399434
ISBN-13: 9781500399436

About the Author

In his live CPE training sessions, Jeff Lenning, CPA CITP, has shown thousands of CPAs and accounting professionals across the country how to use Excel to streamline their work and become more efficient. His Excel articles have been featured in several publications, including the *Journal of Accountancy* and *California CPA Magazine*. He is the founder of Click Consulting, Inc., a firm that specializes in Excel training, consulting, and development. Jeff graduated from the University of Southern California.

EXCEL UNIVERSITY RESOURCES

EXCEL UNIVERSITY WEBSITE

- ✓ excel-university.com

EXCEL UNIVERSITY VIDEO LIBRARY

- ✓ excel-university.com/videos

EXCEL UNIVERSITY DOWNLOAD LIBRARY

- ✓ excel-university.com/downloads

EXCEL UNIVERSITY BLOG

- ✓ excel-university.com/blog

INTERACTIVE ONLINE TRAINING VERSION OF THIS VOLUME

- ✓ excel-university.com/training

Contents at a Glance

Table of Contents

OPENING INFORMATION

*Excel is my favorite computer application of all time.
My goal is to help you maximize its power.*

Chapter 1: Overview

WELCOME BACK!

I'm so glad you've decided to continue on to the next volume in the Excel University series. We covered the foundations in Volume 1, hands-free reporting in Volume 2, and now, in Volume 3, it's time to explore PivotTables.

The first section in this volume is dedicated to PivotTable Fundamentals. We'll cover the basics and work hands-on to build more than 20 PivotTables. In the last chapter of the section, we'll rebuild the final formula-based report of Volume 2 without writing a single formula!

In the second section, Working with PivotTables, we'll explore more PivotTable details and capabilities. This is a fun section because we'll create many formula-based reports and then reproduce them using the PivotTable feature. This approach will ensure you are comfortable replacing formula-based reports with PivotTables when appropriate.

In the final section, Obtain > Prepare > Summarize, we'll examine options for retrieving data from a wide variety of sources and transforming it into the format needed to build summary reports. Finally, we'll review ways to communicate information graphically using various Excel features, including PivotCharts.

BOOK CONVENTIONS

Let's quickly review the conventions used throughout the Excel University series.

REFERENCES

You'll encounter the following references throughout the text:

XREF—a cross-reference to a related or complementary item

NOTE—a general note about the item being presented

KB—the keyboard shortcut or shortcuts used to perform the task

PRACTICE—a reference to the exercise workbook and worksheet

VIDEO—a reference to the related video content

STYLE CONVENTIONS

Formulas are presented in monospaced font, as follows:

```
=SUM(A1:A10)
```

Any additional information about the formula or function is explained immediately after the formula.

FORMULA EVALUATION SEQUENCES

Formula evaluation sequences illustrate the logical steps of a formula. The idea is that the same formula is repeated on many lines with a portion of the formula being evaluated on each line. Throughout this book, I'll underline a portion of the formula in question, show the evaluated result on the next line, and so on. For example, assuming *A1* has a stored value of 100 and *B1* has a stored value of 150, a sample formula evaluation sequence would show as follows:

```
=IF(A1=B1, "OK", B1-A1)
=IF(FALSE, "OK", B1-A1)
=IF(FALSE, "OK", 150-100)
=IF(FALSE, "OK", 50)
=50
```

NOTE

Evaluation sequences are for illustration purposes and are not necessarily the same steps used by Excel's calculation engine. The spaces in the formula above are not needed but have been included to make our first formula evaluation sequence easy to read.

CHAPTER STRUCTURE

In general the chapters that follow contain these sections:

- Set Up—provides an overview and highlights the benefits and uses

- How To—details how to implement the feature or function

- Examples—suggests hands-on exercises that illustrate an application of the feature or function

CORRECTIONS AND SUGGESTIONS

If you have any suggestions or find any errors, please let me know by sending a note to info@excel-university.com.

EXCEL CONVENTIONS

Throughout this text, I've referred to navigation through the Ribbon user interface as follows:

Ribbon Tab Name > Button Name

EXCEL VERSIONS

The screenshots in this volume were captured from Microsoft Excel 2013 for Windows. Not all features and functions discussed in this text are available in older versions of Excel. Additionally, some items presented in this text may not be available in Excel for Mac.

HOW TO MAKE THE MOST

To make the most of our time together, and maximize the benefits of working through the Excel University series, you'll want to be sure to download the sample Excel files and reference the video library as needed. Let's briefly dig into the details.

WORKBOOK DOWNLOAD

In my opinion, the best way to learn Excel is through hands-on experience, and I have provided sample Excel workbooks you can use to gain that experience. Each workbook has a worksheet named Start Here, which lists each exercise and its purpose. The exercise sheets are incomplete. You will complete the exercises by writing a formula or function, or using a feature. These workbooks aren't provided as a reference—rather, they are designed for you to work through and complete. The exercises attempt to demonstrate the application of each feature and function in a relevant and practical way. Please feel free to download the workbooks from the following URL:

www.excel-university.com/downloads

Answers Version

You'll notice that there are essentially two versions of each workbook:

- The exercise version is referenced by name in this text, and provides space to write the formulas and otherwise complete various exercises included in the workbook.

- The answers version is denoted with *_answers* appended to the workbook name, and contains the completed exercises.

Extra Credit

Some exercise workbooks have Extra Credit worksheets. The sheets named Exercise are demonstrated in this text, while the Extra Credit worksheets carry the feature beyond what is presented, providing additional examples and illustrations. The answers for the Extra Credit exercises are included in the answers version of each workbook.

VIDEO LIBRARY

While I did my best to write narrative text that thoroughly explains each topic, video can sometimes be more effective. The Excel University Video Library provides solutions to all exercises in video format, and can be referenced as you work through the book at the following URL:

www.excel-university/videos

MY FAVORITES

As you progress through this volume, it may be helpful to list the items that are the most relevant to you and that you want to implement into your workbooks. Feel free to make notes of those items in the My Favorites table that follows.

MY FAVORITES

Feel free to make a note of features or functions you want to remember to practice and implement into your workbooks as you work through the content.

PAGE	TOPIC

PAGE	TOPIC

PAGE	TOPIC

Chapter 2: Selected Shortcuts

SET UP

I hope you've been using the shortcuts we discussed in the previous volumes. If so, your muscles have memorized them, and they are now second nature.

In this volume, we'll primarily work with Excel features. Since features often utilize dialog boxes, we'll examine the following keyboard shortcuts to help interact with dialog boxes more quickly:

1. Ctrl+PageUp/PageDown

2. Alt Key

3. Tab Key

4. Arrow Keys

5. Letters

Let's see how each of these shortcuts operates within dialog boxes.

HOW TO

As we explore the shortcut keys, we'll reference the Format Cells dialog box shown in Figure 1 below.

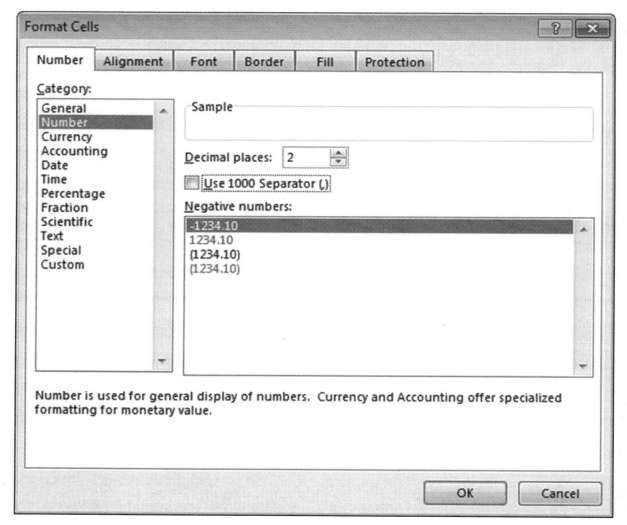

Figure 1

You may ultimately prefer to format cells with Ribbon icons, but because the Format Cells dialog box has such a wide variety of controls, we'll use it to discuss ways to navigate through dialog boxes in general.

CTRL+PAGEUP/PAGEDOWN

When a dialog box has multiple tabs, such as Number, Alignment, Font, Border, Fill, and Protection, we can use the Ctrl+PageUp/PageDown keys to cycle through the tabs. Since these are the same shortcuts we previously explored in Volume 1 to cycle through worksheet tabs, they should feel familiar and intuitive.

ALT KEY

When you look closely at dialog boxes, you'll notice that many of the field labels have an underlined character, such as Category and Decimal places. If you hold down the Alt key while pressing the underlined letter key, you can activate the corresponding dialog option.

TAB KEY

The Tab key moves you forward sequentially through the dialog controls. The currently selected control is typically highlighted in some manner, such as by the thin dotted border around the thousands separator checkbox shown in Figure 1. Shift+Tab moves in reverse.

ARROW KEYS

The arrow keys help select the value for various controls, such as moving up and down the Category list box, and increasing and decreasing the value in the Decimal places option. You can use the arrow keys with many different control types, including tab controls and combo boxes, so feel free to explore.

LETTERS

The letters on your keyboard are a quick way to make selections in certain controls, such as the Category list control. Pressing a letter on your keyboard will advance the selection to the next choice with a matching first letter. Pressing the same letter multiple times continues to advance through choices with matching first letters. For example, pressing C while in the Category field will jump to the Currency choice, and pressing C again will jump down to the Custom choice.

In addition to the letters on your keyboard, the Space bar toggles certain control types, such as checking and unchecking the thousands separator checkbox.

Before we get to the exercises, let's talk about opening and closing dialog boxes. Often, you can open a dialog box by using either a keyboard shortcut or your mouse. To close a dialog box and save changes, use the OK button or the Enter key. To close the dialog box without saving changes, use the Cancel button or the Esc key.

For the most part, it's faster to interact with dialog boxes by using the keyboard, although there are times when clicking a Ribbon icon may be the fastest way to complete your task. For dialog boxes you use frequently, you'll find that you can quickly navigate with a keyboard because you'll naturally memorize the keystroke sequence needed to complete your task.

 XREF

For a comprehensive list of shortcuts covered in the Excel University series to date, please refer to the Shortcut Reference near the end of the book.

EXAMPLES

Let's practice with a few hands-on exercises.

 **PRACTICE**

To work along, please refer to *Selected Shortcuts.xlsx*.

 VIDEO

To watch the solutions video, please visit the Excel University Video Library.

EXERCISE 1—FORMAT CELLS

In this exercise, we'll use our keyboard to format a range of cells.

 **PRACTICE**

To work along, please refer to the Exercise 1 worksheet.

Our transaction data includes an Amount column that we need to format as currency, with no decimals, a comma for thousands, and the $ currency symbol.

We select the range and then open the Format Cells dialog box.

 KB

With the Format Cells dialog open, we can use Ctrl+PageUp/PageDown to navigate to the Number tab if needed.

Then we select the Category list box by pressing Tab, or Alt+C. We select Currency from the list with the Down Arrow key, or with the letter C on the keyboard.

We select the Decimal places field with Tab, or Alt+D. We specify no decimals by using the Down Arrow key, or by typing 0.

It probably feels like formatting cells this way takes longer than with the mouse, but navigating through frequently used dialog boxes with your keyboard will get pretty fast over time.

EXERCISE 2—CENTER ACROSS SELECTION

In this exercise, we'll use our keyboard to center a label over four cells.

 **PRACTICE**

To work along, please refer to the Exercise 2 worksheet.

We have a report with four region columns, and want to center the label Regions across the columns. We can accomplish this by using the Center Across Selection alignment option.

We select the Regions label cell plus the remaining three empty cells to the right and then open the Format Cells dialog box.

Using Ctrl+PageUp/PageDown, we navigate to the Alignment tab.

We navigate to the Horizontal field by pressing Tab or Alt+H and then hit either the Down Arrow key or the letter C until the Center Across Selection option is selected.

We close the dialog box by pressing Enter.

EXERCISE 3—NAMED REFERENCE

In this exercise, we'll use our keyboard to define a named reference.

 **PRACTICE**

> To work along, please refer to the Exercise 3 worksheet.

We allow the user to enter a rate, such as 5%, into the input cell *C8*. To make it easy to use the rate throughout the workbook, let's assign a name, such as **rate,** to the input cell.

Select the input cell and then open the Name Manager dialog box.

 KB

> Open the Name Manager dialog box with Ctrl+F3; Alt+I, N, D (insert, name, define); or Alt+M, N (formulas, name manager).

In the Name Manager dialog, use Alt+N to activate the new name button. In the New Name dialog, type the desired name and press Enter to save changes and close the dialog. You are returned to the Name Manager dialog and can confirm the new name appears in the list. Close the Name Manager dialog by selecting the Close button or by hitting the Esc key.

 NOTE

> You won't lose your new name by using the Esc key to close the Name Manager dialog since the name was created with the New Name dialog, not the Name Manager dialog.

EXERCISE 4—DATA VALIDATION

In this exercise, we'll use data validation to create a drop-down box.

 **PRACTICE**

> To work along, please refer to the Exercise 4 worksheet.

On the *E4 Data* sheet, we store a list of regions in a table named *Table1*. In the input cell on the *Exercise 4* worksheet, we'll present these regions in a drop-down box.

Since the data validation feature doesn't directly support structured table references, let's set up a name, *regions*, which refers to the cells in the table. We select the table's region cells, being careful to exclude the column header. Using the shortcuts discussed in the previous exercise, we assign the name *regions* to the selected table column.

 XREF

Using data validation with tables and named references is discussed in Volume 1, Chapter 9.

We flip to the *Exercise 4* sheet to set up data validation. We select the region input cell and open the Data Validation dialog box.

 KB

Open the Data Validation dialog box with Alt+D, L (<u>d</u>ata, va<u>l</u>idation) or Alt+A, V, V (d<u>a</u>ta, data <u>v</u>alidation, data <u>v</u>alidation).

In the Data Validation dialog box, we activate the Allow field by pressing Tab or Alt+A. We select List with the Down Arrow key or the L key. We activate the Source field by pressing Tab or Alt+S. We type in the source value *=regions*.

 KB

Rather than type the name, we could open the Paste Name dialog box using the F3 key, select the name with the arrow keys, and hit Enter to paste it.

We close the dialog box by pressing Enter, and bam, the input cell now has a drop-down box.

CHAPTER CONCLUSION

At first, navigating through dialog boxes using keyboard shortcuts may feel cumbersome, but with some practice you'll be able to open and close your frequently used dialog boxes in a flash.

PIVOTTABLE FUNDAMENTALS

Pivot Table Warm-Up

Chapter 3: PivotTable Basics

SET UP

The PivotTable (PT) feature is one of my favorites, and I'm excited to explore it with you! It is a big feature with many details to unpack. We'll take our time and work through it methodically so that you'll be comfortable creating PivotTable reports. Wait, what was that? Yes, PivotTable *reports*. A PivotTable is a report. The PivotTable feature creates PivotTable reports.

We spent a ton of time in Volume 2 creating formula-based reports using the SUMIFS function. Many of those reports could have been built with the PivotTable feature … many, but not all. The formula-based reports had virtually no structure limits. We built summary reports and financial statements, and placed each report label and value into the desired cells. The structure of PivotTable reports is not as flexible as formula-based reports. While PivotTables are great for aggregation and analysis, they are not a good fit for complex reports such as financial statements containing rigid layout and formatting requirements.

Let's take a look at the final report we built in Volume 2, shown in Figure 2 below.

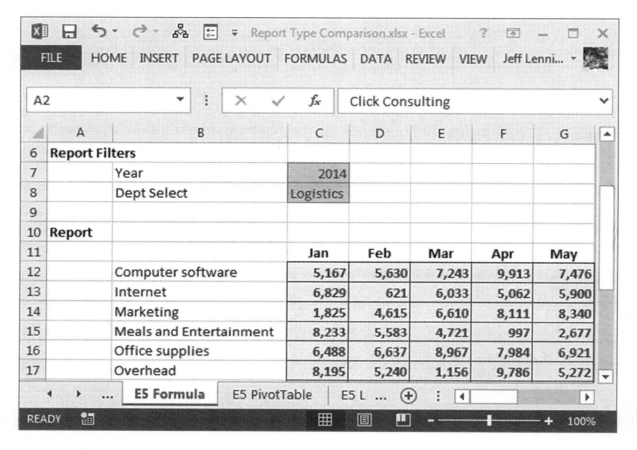

Figure 2

Let's examine the report layout for a moment. The report *rows* display the accounts, such as Computer software, Internet, and Marketing. The report *columns* display the months. The report *values* are the subtotaled transaction amounts. There are report *filters* for year and department.

Recognizing that the report can be described by the content displayed in these four areas (rows, columns, values, and filters) will come in handy when we recreate the report using the PivotTable feature. We created the formula-based version of this report at the end of Volume 2, and we'll create the corresponding PivotTable report by the end of the first section of this volume.

Let's check out the PivotTable version of the report, shown in Figure 3 below.

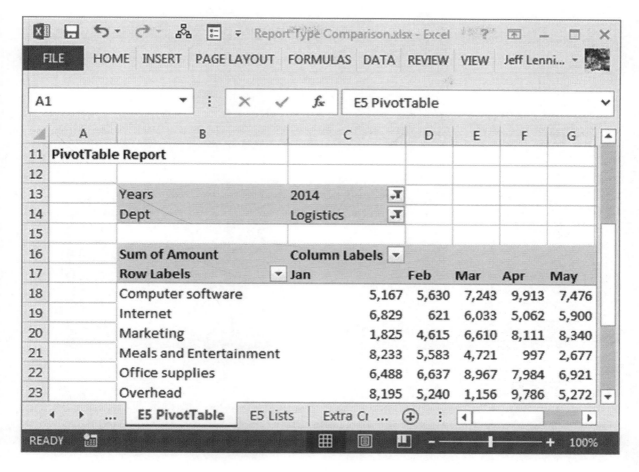

Figure 3

This report was built without writing a single formula! It was created by interactively defining the report structure using the PivotTable feature. Let's explore the mechanics now.

HOW TO

PivotTable reports summarize data, and the data source may contain several columns or fields. After visualizing the desired report, you insert a new PivotTable into the worksheet. You define the basic report structure simply by inserting fields into the layout areas, rows, columns, values, and filters. With that basic overview in mind, let's explore the details by creating a department report from transactions we exported from our accounting system.

DATA

Let's start by examining the transactions we want to summarize. Our data source is shown in Figure 4 below.

	B	C	D	E	F	G	H
11	TransID	AcctNum	Account	DeptNum	Dept	Date	Amount
12	4821	5052	Postage	202	Research	1/1/2014	2,140
13	4822	5050	Computer ‹	202	Research	1/13/2014	616
14	4823	5020	Wages	202	Research	1/26/2014	2,761
15	4824	5054	Internet	202	Research	1/20/2014	2,508
16	4825	5041	Trade show	202	Research	1/17/2014	4,891

Figure 4

The first thing to note is that the data is flat. Earlier in the Excel University series, we described the characteristics of flat data and discussed the benefits of using it with Excel.

 XREF

Flat data is described in Volume 1, Chapter 16.

Since the PivotTable feature is designed to summarize flat data, you'll want to start with a nice, flat data range that contains values in all cells and does not contain blank rows or columns.

 XREF

If you need to flatten your data, try the steps discussed in Chapter 24: Data Preparation.

Note also that our source data includes column headers, such as TransID, AcctNum, and Account. The PivotTable feature is designed to work with source data that stores column headers in a single worksheet row.

With the data source ready to go, we can insert a new PivotTable.

INSERT PIVOTTABLE

Wanting to summarize the data by department, we visualize a report with department and amount columns.

After selecting any single cell in the data source range, we use the following Ribbon command to open the Create PivotTable dialog shown in Figure 5 below.

- Insert > PivotTable

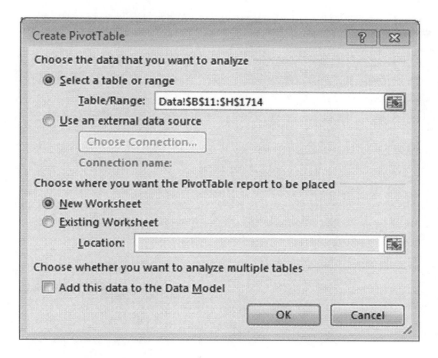

Figure 5

Excel needs two pieces of information, the location of the data we want to analyze and the location of the PivotTable. If the data is stored in the workbook, we select the appropriate table or range. If the data is stored outside of the workbook, we specify an external data source. Our data is stored in the workbook, so we specify the worksheet range. If we select a cell within the data source range before opening the dialog, Excel populates the range automatically, as shown above. Otherwise we can select or enter the range manually.

Excel also needs to know if the report should be placed in a new or existing worksheet. If new, Excel will insert a new worksheet. If existing, Excel will need the location.

 NOTE

The existing worksheet location field expects a cell reference, not a worksheet reference. Be sure to select a cell within the destination sheet.

Since we want our report to be placed on an existing worksheet, we select the desired worksheet cell to designate the upper-left corner of the report. The updated dialog box is shown in Figure 6 below.

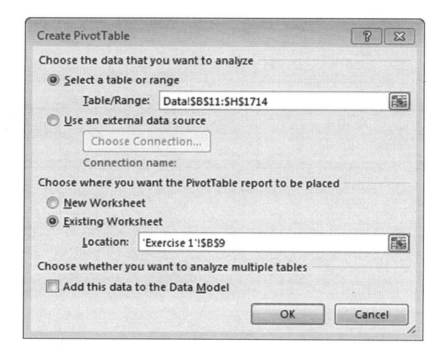

Figure 6

Once we identify the locations of both the data and the report, we click OK to insert the PivotTable. Let's take a moment to examine some of the resulting changes to our worksheet, shown in Figure 7 below.

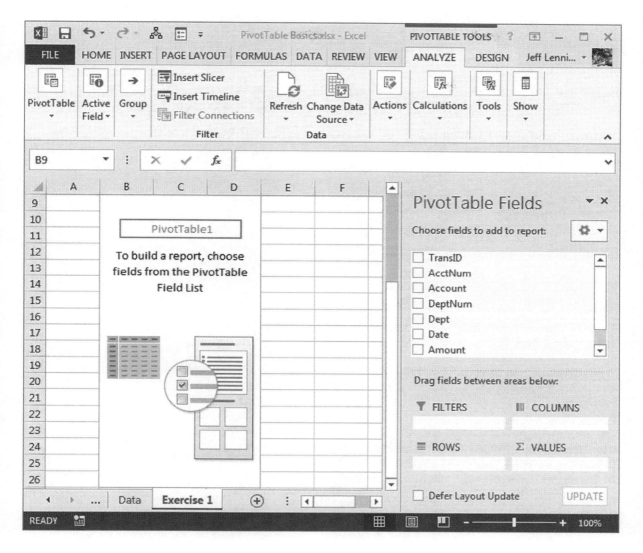

Figure 7

A new graphic was inserted at the specified report location, in our case, cell **B9**. The graphic is a temporary placeholder and will disappear once we begin building the report.

A new PivotTable Tools tab appeared in the Ribbon. This tab is displayed as needed, and it is needed to manage the active PivotTable. If it disappears, just activate the PivotTable again by selecting any cell within the report. We'll explore this tab's many icons and options during the course of this volume.

A new PivotTable Fields panel appeared and, similar to the Ribbon tab, is displayed as needed. It is needed to define the report. Notice the panel is split into two parts. The top half contains a list of fields with checkboxes. If we take a moment to compare the fields shown in Figure 7 with the source data shown in Figure 4, we'll see that the fields represent data columns. The bottom half of the panel includes the four areas we use to define the structure: rows, columns, values, and filters. Do these areas sound familiar? When we were examining the report in Figure 2, we recognized that the report could be described by what was displayed in these four areas. We will define the report simply by inserting fields into the layout areas.

 NOTE

The Field list panel appears when a PivotTable is active, unless you have hidden it. For example, clicking the X in the upper-right corner will permanently toggle off its display. If this happens, the panel will not appear when you activate a PivotTable, and you'll need to toggle it back on by clicking the Field List Ribbon icon.

 NOTE

The default field panel is split as described and referenced throughout this text. The settings icon in the upper-right corner of the panel reveals several alternatives.

DEFINING THE REPORT STRUCTURE

To define our department report, we just need to insert the correct fields into the correct areas. Knowing which fields to insert into which areas will take a little practice, so let me describe how I remember what goes where when building PivotTables.

I start by listening for the keyword *by* because it usually indicates row fields. For example, I may want to see a report *by* department or *by* customer. This keyword suggests that the field belongs in the rows area. If you want to see the report *by* department, then the department field belongs in the rows area. If you want to see it *by* account, then the account field belongs in the rows area.

Next, I identify numeric data columns because they usually represent value fields. For example, I may want to add an amount or quantity column. To build a report that shows the amount by department, you insert the department field into the rows area and the amount field into the values area.

I then consider column fields, which spread values across columns. For example, I may want to see one column for each department. To build a report that shows each account's amount spread across departments, you insert the account field into the rows area, the amount field into the values area, and the department field into the columns area.

Last, I think about report filters. For example, I may want to view transactions for a specific department. The filters area allows you to control which data rows flow into the report. To build a report that shows the amount by account and provides a filter for departments, you would insert the account field into the rows area, the amount field into the values area, and the department field into the filters area.

Now that we have a general idea of which fields belong in which areas, let's review several common ways to place fields into report areas. You can click and drag the field into the area, right-click the field and select the desired report area, or check the field's checkbox. If you check the checkbox, Excel inserts the field by guessing the most appropriate area. You can always drag and drop the field to the correct area if needed.

 NOTE

Excel guesses the most appropriate area using simple logic. If all cells in the data column contain numbers, the field will be placed into the values area; otherwise the field will be placed into the rows area.

Let's wrap up by completing our department report. Since we want to show amount by department, we insert the department field into the rows area and the amount field into the values area. We are presented with the report shown in Figure 8 below.

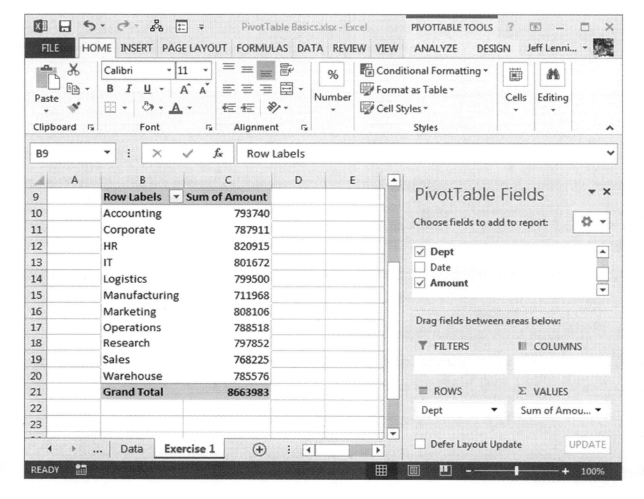

Figure 8

Since we wanted to summarize the data by department, we initially visualized a report with department and amount columns. Even though we didn't write any formulas, here it is!

Are you ready to try? I would encourage you to complete the exercises presented in this book. To get good at driving a car, you can't just read about it, you have to get behind the wheel. The same holds true with Excel. So now is the perfect time to download the files, open Excel, and get ready to drive.

EXAMPLES

Please work through the following exercises.

To work along, please refer to *PivotTable Basics.xlsx.*

To watch the solutions video, please visit the Excel University Video Library.

EXERCISE 1—AMOUNT BY DEPARTMENT

Let's warm up by building a simple department report.

PRACTICE

To work along, please refer to the Exercise 1 worksheet.

We've exported some transactions from our accounting system, and we want to build a report that computes the amount by department. If we tried to visualize what we want the report to look like, we see a row for each department and a column containing the total amount for each department. With that picture in mind, we begin.

The transactions stored on the *Data* worksheet will be used as the PivotTable data source. We flip to the *Data* sheet, select a single cell in the source data range, and open the Create PivotTable dialog box by selecting the following Ribbon icon:

- Insert > PivotTable

In the resulting Create PivotTable dialog box, we confirm the prepopulated data range is accurate and opt to place the PivotTable in an existing worksheet by selecting the Existing Worksheet radio button. We then navigate to the *Exercise 1* worksheet and select cell *B9*. We click OK to insert the PivotTable into the worksheet.

Since we want to see the amounts by department, we know we need to insert the department field into the rows area and the amount field into the values area. We check the department field's checkbox to insert it into the rows area, and the results are shown in Figure 9 below.

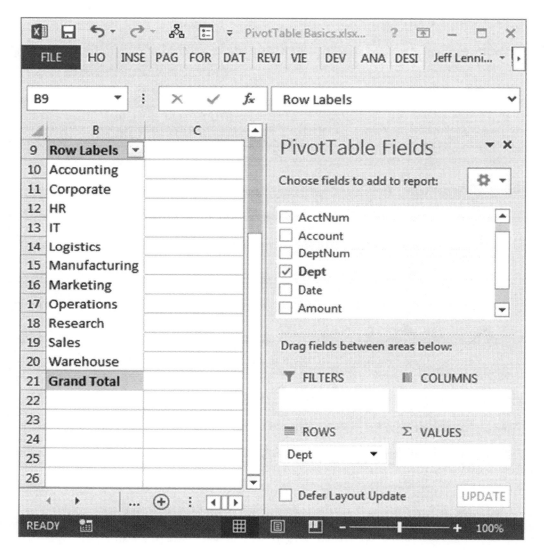

Figure 9

Although the data included many transactions for each department, the report includes only a single row for each department. Row fields create one row for each unique field value.

We insert the amount field into the values area by checking the checkbox, and the updated PivotTable is shown in Figure 10 below.

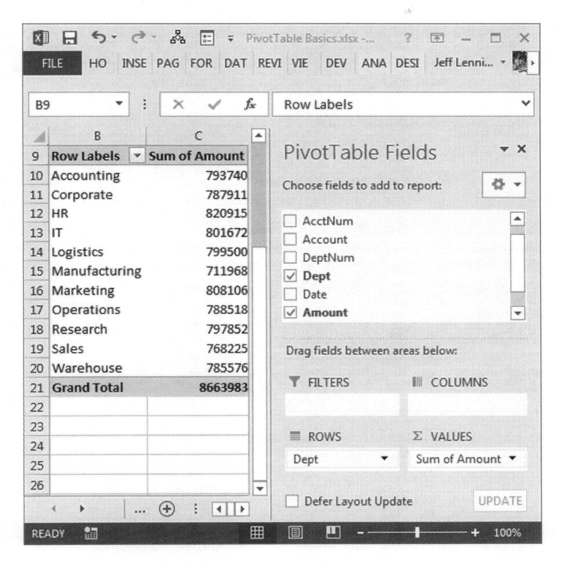

Figure 10

Hey, congratulations … you just built a PivotTable!

EXERCISE 2—AMOUNT BY ACCOUNT

In this exercise, we'll build a report that provides totals by account.

 **PRACTICE**

To work along, please refer to the Exercise 2 worksheet.

We need to summarize the data on the **Data** worksheet by account. Visualizing the report before we start, we imagine a report with account and amount columns.

We flip to the **Data** sheet, select any cell in the data range, and open the Create PivotTable dialog box.

In the Create PivotTable dialog, we confirm the source data range is accurate and opt to insert the PivotTable in an existing worksheet by selecting the Existing Worksheet radio button, navigating to the **Exercise 2** worksheet, and selecting cell **B9**. We click OK to insert the PivotTable into the worksheet.

We know we need to insert the account field into the rows area, so we check the corresponding checkbox in the field list, and confirm that Excel inserted it as expected. We insert the amount field into the report by checking its checkbox. The resulting PivotTable is shown in Figure 11 below.

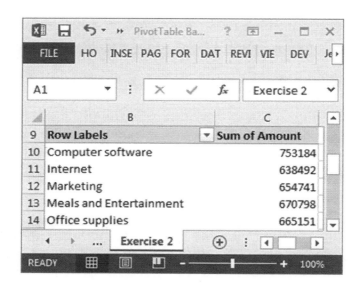

Figure 11

The resulting PivotTable report summarizes the data by account, just like we wanted.

CHAPTER CONCLUSION

A PivotTable is simply a report that summarizes data. You assign fields to define the report rows, columns, values, and filters. The remainder of this volume builds on the basic ideas presented in this chapter, so be sure that you complete the chapter exercises ... they only get harder from here! You'll build more than 60 PivotTables if you complete all of the exercises in this volume. Remember: drill for skill.

Chapter 4: Row Fields

SET UP

We need to discuss a few details about row fields. Let's pretend we had some sales transactions in a worksheet and wanted to view a report that showed sales by region, and then within each region, by rep. There's that keyword *by* again. Viewing sales *by* region *by* rep implies that we need two row fields. Can a PivotTable have two row fields? Yes! Fortunately, it is easy to insert multiple fields into the rows area. Let's work through this and a few other row field mechanics now.

HOW TO

This chapter is designed to discuss a few of the subtle details you need to know about working with row fields. We'll discuss the following items:

- Multiple row fields

- Order matters

- Remove a field

- Expand and collapse

- Unique rows

- Report structure conventions

Let's work through each of these items briefly.

MULTIPLE ROW FIELDS

Creating a PivotTable with multiple row fields is easy; we just insert them, one after the other, into the rows area. For example, if we need to view the report by region by rep, we insert region, then rep, into the rows area. No big deal.

ORDER MATTERS

It is important to realize that order matters. Inserting the region field and then the rep field into the rows area produces a report that shows sales by region, and then within each region shows sales by rep. Inserting the rep field and then the region field produces a report that shows sales by rep, and then within each rep shows sales by region. With that said, we need to distinguish between chronological order and field order.

Chronological order is the order in which we place the fields into the report, and field order is the order in which they appear in the report. These orders may or may not be the same. If we insert fields by using the checkboxes, then the chronological order typically is the same as the field order because Excel automatically places row fields under any existing row fields. However, if we click and drag the fields, we can place them into the report in any order and move around their order at any time.

Assuming we insert rep and then region, our rows area would appear as shown in Figure 12 below.

Figure 12

If we wanted to see the report by region, and then within each region by rep, we could reposition the order by clicking and dragging the fields to create the updated rows area shown in Figure 13 below.

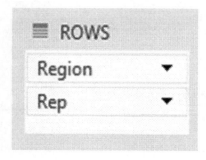

Figure 13

Keep in mind that order matters, and that you can reposition the field order anytime.

REMOVE A FIELD

Once you've inserted a field into a PivotTable, you can easily remove it by unchecking its checkbox or clicking and dragging it out of the layout area.

EXPAND AND COLLAPSE

When a PivotTable contains multiple row fields, you can expand and collapse detail. For example, if you have region and rep fields, you can collapse and hide the rep detail. To expand and collapse a field label, click its +/- icon, double-click the cell, or right-click the cell and select Expand or Collapse from the shortcut menu.

In addition to toggling individual labels, you can expand/collapse all labels for a field at the same type by right-clicking a label and selecting Expand Entire Field or Collapse Entire Field, or by selecting the following Ribbon icon:

- PivotTable Tools > Analyze > Expand Field
- PivotTable Tools > Analyze > Collapse Field

As you can see, it's easy to show and hide detail as needed.

UNIQUE ROWS

Do you remember how we generated unique report labels when we were building formula-based reports in Volume 2? We started with the source data and then used the remove duplicates feature to create a list of unique report labels. The PivotTable feature performs this task automatically by creating one row for each unique field item.

REPORT STRUCTURE CONVENTION

We'll build a lot of PivotTables during this volume, and the following convention will efficiently communicate the report structure. Since PivotTables can be described by which fields are placed into which areas, I will identify the PivotTable area in caps and then indicate the field or fields. For example, to indicate a PT that reports amount by department and by account, I'll use:

- PT ROWS: Department, Account; VALUES: Amount

Now, it is time to get busy.

EXAMPLES

Let's try a few hands-on exercises at this point.

 **PRACTICE**

To work along, please refer to *Row Fields.xlsx.*

 VIDEO

To watch the solutions video, please visit the Excel University Video Library.

EXERCISE 1—TWO ROW FIELDS

In this exercise, we'll build a PivotTable with two row fields and then show and hide detail.

 **PRACTICE**

To work along, please refer to the Exercise 1 worksheet.

We've exported sales transactions from our accounting system, and the data contains TransID, Region, Rep, Item, Date, and Amount columns. We want to summarize the data by region and within each region by rep, so we build the following report:

- PT ROWS: Region, Rep; VALUES: Amount

Now that our basic report is done, let's try to hide the detail for the first region. We can double-click the region label worksheet cell or use one of the other methods discussed above. Double-click it again to expand it.

Now, let's collapse all regions at once. We select a region cell and then use the right-click shortcut menu or the Ribbon icon discussed above. We can use a similar technique to easily expand all regions at once.

EXERCISE 2—THREE ROW FIELDS

In this exercise, we'll build a PivotTable with three row fields and play with the field order.

 **PRACTICE**

To work along, please refer to the Exercise 2 worksheet.

We'd like to analyze the same sales data, but now we'd like to view sales by item. We build the following report:

- PT ROWS: Item; VALUES: Amount

Looks good. But now we want to view sales by item, and then within each item, we want to see which regions have sales. So we modify the report by inserting the region field as follows:

- PT ROWS: Item, Region; VALUES: Amount

Looks good. But now all of a sudden we want to analyze sales by region, and then within each region, by item. All we need to do is switch the order of the row labels as follows:

- PT ROWS: Region, Item; VALUES: Amount

Looks good. But now, we want to analyze sales by region, and then within each region by rep, and then within each rep, by item. So, we simply insert the rep field as follows:

- PT ROWS: Region, Rep, Item; VALUES: Amount

We are able to quickly summarize and view the data in different ways by positioning the row fields as desired.

CHAPTER CONCLUSION

The objective of this chapter was to discuss row field details, such as how to insert multiple row fields, remove them, and expand and collapse them. We've also discovered how row fields automatically generate a unique list of items.

Chapter 5: Value Fields

SET UP

Have you noticed that every time we've inserted a field into the values area, Excel automatically summed the values? If you think about this for a moment, you'll realize that Excel guessed that we wanted to sum the values. But what if we wanted to find the average, the count, or the maximum value? We can do this easily because we can apply a variety of math functions to value fields. This chapter discusses the logic Excel uses to guess the most appropriate function and then demonstrates how to set the desired function.

HOW TO

Value fields typically summarize numeric data, but the PivotTable feature supports non-numeric value fields as well. Based on the column's data type, Excel tries to determine the most appropriate math function. Do you remember Excel guessed the area when we inserted a field by checking its checkbox? Excel applied simple logic to make a guess. If the data source column was completely filled with numbers, then Excel placed the field in the values area; otherwise it placed the field in the rows area. The logic Excel uses to guess which math to apply to value fields is similar. If the column is completely filled with numbers, then Excel uses the sum function; otherwise it uses the count function.

Now that we understand the logic behind Excel's guesses, let's control the math used to summarize a value field. Each PivotTable field has numerous settings, and Excel provides two dialog boxes to manage them. The Value Field Settings dialog is displayed for value fields, and the Field Settings dialog is displayed for row, column, and filter fields. The Value Field Settings dialog box (Figure 14) is explored in this chapter, and the Field Settings dialog box (Figure 27) is explored in an upcoming chapter.

You can open the Value Field Settings dialog box by right-clicking any value cell and then selecting Value Field Settings from the shortcut menu; by clicking the field control in the report layout area and then Value Field Settings from the shortcut menu; or by selecting any value cell and then the following Ribbon command:

- PivotTable Tools > Analyze > Field Settings

All of these methods open the Value Field Settings dialog, as shown in Figure 14 below.

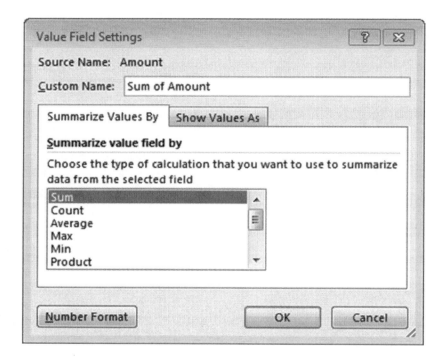

Figure 14

You'll notice the following items in the dialog box:

- Custom Name field—use this to rename the field label

- Summarize Values By tab—use this to define the math function

- Show Values As tab—use this to select additional display options

- Number Format button—use this to format the value field

The Number Format button is discussed in Chapter 10: Value Formats. The Show Values As tab is discussed in Chapter 17: Show Values As.

To change the math used to summarize the values, simply select the desired function in the Value Field Settings dialog box and click OK. The updated report values, which are stored values, not formulas, will be displayed. In addition to specifying the math through the Value Field Settings dialog box, you can also right-click any value cell and select Summarize Values By from the shortcut menu.

UPDATED REPORT STRUCTURE CONVENTION

Now that we understand how to select different functions to summarize value fields, we'll update our convention to include the desired function. For example, to indicate that we want to sum the amount field, we'll use:

- PT ROWS: Department; VALUES: Sum(Amount)

To indicate that we want to count the amount field, we'll use:

- PT ROWS: Department; VALUES: Count(Amount)

Eventually, we'll discover that we can group date fields. To indicate that we want to group the date field by month, we'll use:

- PT ROWS: Month(Date); VALUES: Sum(Amount)

Even though the month group isn't technically a function, this notation provides a convenient way to communicate the desired group option.

Date groups are discussed in Chapter 9: Groups and Subtotals.

This convention will carry us through the remainder of the volume.

CHANGING HEADER LABELS

By default, Excel names value field headers with the function and then the field name. For example, if we use the count function on the ItemNum field, the PivotTable report will display "Count of ItemNum" for the column header. There are several ways to change PivotTable header labels. You can open up the Field Settings dialog box and change the Custom Name field value, you can simply type the desired label into the cell, or you can select any cell for the field and enter the desired name into the following Ribbon field:

- PivotTable Tools > Analyze > Active Field

Note that some restrictions apply to renaming PivotTable labels. For example, you can't reuse an existing field name. If you have a conflict with an existing field name, a common approach is to add a trailing space to the PivotTable label. Changing the default headers can help clean up and clarify our reports.

 NOTE

In addition to changing report headers, we can also change row and column labels. For example, we can change an account row label from Meals and Entertainment to M&E. In practice, I try to avoid doing this, since it makes tying the report back to the data more difficult because the report labels and data labels will no longer match. We can hide headers with the following Ribbon icon:

- PivotTable Tools > Analyze > Field Headers

DRILL DOWN

We have the ability to drill down into value fields. When we double-click a value cell, Excel displays that cell's related transactions in a newly inserted sheet. We can navigate back to the report by deleting the detail sheet or switching back to the PivotTable sheet using the mouse or keyboard.

 XREF

By default, drill down (Enable Show Details) is enabled, but you can disable it in the PivotTable Options dialog box, discussed in Chapter 12: Options.

While this is a great way for us to understand and research report values, it is also helpful when we deliver digital reports. Our report users can drill into the detail for any value simply by double-clicking the cell. If we think about this idea for a moment, we'll quickly realize that a report user could drill into many values and thus create many extra worksheets. Will these new sheets be saved and displayed to the next report user? Yes, unless we prevent it.

One easy way to prevent new sheets from being saved is by enabling the read-only file attribute. In Windows Explorer, right-click the file name, open the properties dialog, and set the file to read-only. When set, the user can make changes to the workbook, including adding sheets, but the changes will not be saved. When the workbook is closed, the changes are disregarded, and the next user has a nice, clean report workbook. Please note any user can disable the read-only attribute, and it doesn't prevent a user from deleting the file.

Another way to prevent new sheets from being saved is by using network security. To do this, you place the report files in a network folder that gives you read/write access but gives report users read-only access. If needed, your IT person can help set up a network folder with the correct permissions. In addition to these options, you can use Excel's built-in security features such as workbook protection.

 XREF

Workbook protection is discussed in a subsequent volume.

I can tell you are not nearly excited enough, so let me share a quick story. When I was the accounting manager at a public company, it was my job to deliver monthly Selling, General, and Administrative (SG&A) reports to our department managers. Originally I delivered them as printed reports. When a manager asked a question about a number, I would run to my computer, open our accounting system, run a transaction detail report, filter it for the correct period, department, and account, and then print and deliver it. This was a manual process that happened each month. To automate this recurring process, I started delivering digital SG&A PivotTables instead of printed reports. A manager who had a question about any number could double-click it to view the related transactions. We were all much happier and more efficient, thanks to Excel PivotTables.

I hope you are now excited enough to open the exercise workbook and work on the exercises!

EXAMPLES

We'll practice by completing several exercises.

 **PRACTICE**

To work along, please refer to *Value Fields.xlsx.*

 VIDEO

To watch the solutions video, please visit the Excel University Video Library.

EXERCISE 1—COUNT

In this exercise, we'll use the count function to summarize the amount field.

 **PRACTICE**

To work along, please refer to the Exercise 1 worksheet.

We've exported transactions from our accounting system and stored them on the *E1 Data* sheet. The extract includes TransID, ItemNum, Date, and Amount columns.

Since we want to determine the number of transactions per item, we use the count function to summarize the data. We want to build the following report:

- PT ROWS: ItemNum; VALUES: Count(Amount)

We begin by creating a new PivotTable and inserting the ItemNum field into the rows area. Next, we insert the Amount field into the values area. Since this data column is filled with numbers, Excel assumes we want to use the sum function. However, we want to count the number of transaction rows instead, so we choose the count function in the Value Field Settings dialog, as shown in Figure 15 below.

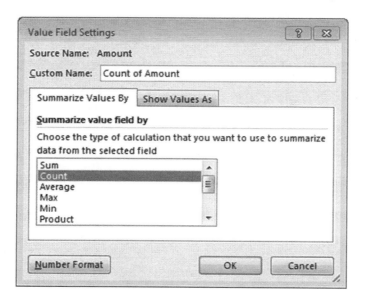

Figure 15

The resulting report is shown in Figure 16 below.

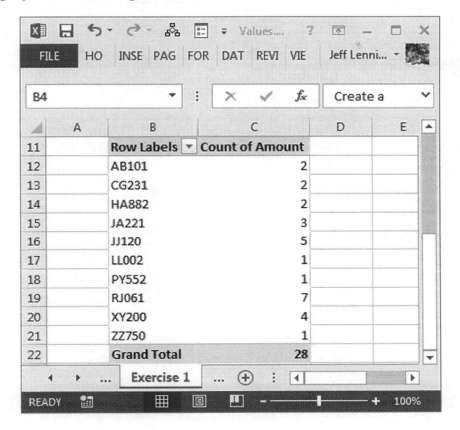

Figure 16

Our report now presents exactly what we want: the number of transactions for each item.

 NOTE

The count function counts the number of nonblank cells. Since we are simply counting the number of cells with values, we could have used any other column as the value field, provided all cells in the column contained a value.

EXERCISE 2—SUM

In this exercise, we'll sum an amount column that includes an empty cell.

 **PRACTICE**

To work along, please refer to the Exercise 2 worksheet.

We've exported some transactions from our accounting system and stored them on the *E2 Data* sheet. This extract is similar to the extract from the previous exercise, except its Amount column includes a blank cell. Cell *E11* is empty, as shown in Figure 17 below.

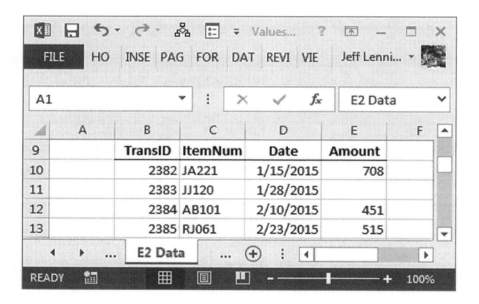

Figure 17

Our goal is to view subtotals by item, so we set out to build the following report:

• PT ROWS: ItemNum; VALUES: Sum(Amount)

Inserting the ItemNum field into the rows area is easy, but we hit a snag when we try to insert the Amount field into the values area. When we check the checkbox, Excel inserts the field into the rows area instead of the values area. Do you know why? It is because the data column is not completely filled with numbers, which is a result of the blank cell. Fortunately, we can easily insert the field into the values area by clicking and dragging. But when we do, Excel automatically uses the count function instead of the desired sum function. Do you know why? Yes, once again it is because of the blank cell. Fortunately, we can easily change the math by opening the settings dialog and selecting the sum function. Ah, yes, much better.

EXERCISE 3—AVERAGE

In this exercise, we'll compute the average transaction amount for each item.

 **PRACTICE**

To work along, please refer to the Exercise 3 worksheet.

We've exported data from our accounting system and stored it in the *E3 Data* sheet. The extract contains TransID, ItemNum, Date, and Amount columns. We are interested in the average transaction amount for each item, so we set out to build the following report:

- PT ROWS: ItemNum; VALUES: Average(Amount)

We easily insert the ItemNum field. When we insert the Amount field, Excel applies the sum function. Fortunately, we know how to change the math. Using one of the techniques discussed above, we apply the average function.

 NOTE

To determine the average, Excel divides the sum of the Amount column by the count of the Amount column. The denominator is the number of cells with values, not the number of rows. This distinction may be important, depending on your goal.

EXERCISE 4—UNIQUE LIST

In this exercise, we'll generate a unique list of items and count the number of times each appears in the data source.

 **PRACTICE**

To work along, please refer to the Exercise 4 worksheet.

We previously explored how to view duplicate values with the conditional formatting feature, and how to remove duplicate items with the remove duplicates feature. Now, we'll identify duplicates and remove them with the PivotTable feature.

 XREF

Conditional formatting is discussed in Volume 1, Chapter 10. Remove duplicates is discussed in Volume 2, Chapter 4.

PivotTable row fields automatically create a unique list of row labels. Previously we used the remove duplicates feature to accomplish this. When we use the count function on a value field, the report identifies the number of times each item appears, and duplicate items are those appearing more than once. Previously we used the conditional formatting feature to identify duplicates. Let's get a unique list of item numbers and compute the number of times each appears by creating the following report:

- PT ROWS: ItemNum; VALUES: Count(ItemNum)

After changing the value field label, our report appears in Figure 18 below.

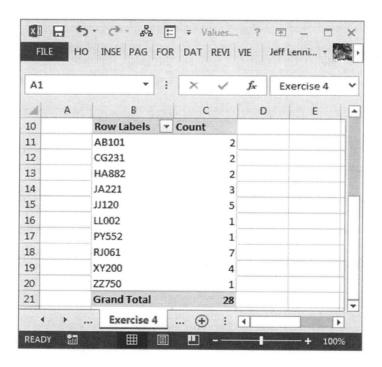

Figure 18

Now let's walk through the detailed steps. We begin by inserting the ItemNum field into the rows area. Next we want to insert the ItemNum field into the values area, but we can't because the checkbox is already checked. No worries, we can insert it by dragging and dropping the field into the values area. Since the field does not contain numbers, Excel automatically defaults the math to count. To clean up the report, we change the value field label from Count of ItemNum to Count.

I like this exercise because it shows how to set up a non-numeric value field and how to insert the same field into the report more than once. Plus, it demonstrates how the PivotTable feature creates a list of unique report labels, which we previously accomplished with the remove duplicates feature. It also identifies the duplicate labels (those with a count greater than one), which we previously accomplished with the conditional formatting feature.

EXERCISE 5—DRILL DOWN

In this exercise, we'll drill down into the details.

 **PRACTICE**

To work along, please refer to the Exercise 5 worksheet.

Let's get started by creating the following report:

- PT ROWS: ItemNum; VALUES: Sum(Amount)

Now double-click any value cell to drill into the detail. Wow! Excel instantly pasted the related transactions into a new worksheet to the left of the report worksheet. If you want to retain the detail sheet, navigate back to the report sheet with your mouse or keyboard. If you are done with the detail sheet, delete it with your mouse or keyboard and you'll automatically arrive back at the report sheet. This capability makes it easy to review reports.

 KB

Delete a sheet with Alt+E, L (edit, delete) or Alt+H, D, S (home, delete, sheet).

CHAPTER CONCLUSION

In this chapter, we explored how to control the function used to summarize value fields, and we are now more comfortable building PivotTables.

Chapter 6: Column Fields

SET UP

So far we have examined row and value fields. It is now time to explore column fields, which create one column for each unique item. For example, we could generate a report that includes a column for each department or a column for each region. Column fields allow us to create crosstab-style reports, where columns reflect subgroups of the data. Column fields are useful when aggregating transactions and when transposing the orientation of data that comes in a vertical orientation.

HOW TO

To create a column field, drag the field into the columns area. For example, to build a report with one column for each department, insert the department field into the columns area, as shown in Figure 19 below.

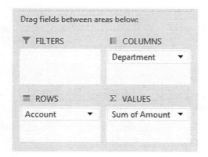

Figure 19

Using our convention, the report would be described as follows:

- PT ROWS: Account; COLUMNS: Department; VALUES: Sum(Amount)

Think you got this? All right then, time to crack open the exercise workbook and give it a try.

EXAMPLES

Let's try a few hands-on exercises to practice inserting column fields.

 **PRACTICE**

To work along, please refer to *Column Fields.xlsx*.

 VIDEO

To watch the solutions video, please visit the Excel University Video Library.

EXERCISE 1—DEPARTMENTS

In this exercise, we'll create a report with one column for each department.

 **PRACTICE**

To work along, please refer to the Exercise 1 worksheet.

We have exported a list of transactions from our accounting system and stored them on the *Data* sheet. The extract includes TransID, AcctNum, Account, DeptNum, Department, Date, and Amount columns. We would like to summarize the data by account and display one column for each department, so we set out to build the following report:

- PT ROWS: Account; COLUMNS: Department; VALUES: Sum(Amount)

In a new PivotTable, we insert the account field into the rows area. We drag the department field into the columns area. We insert the amount field into the values area. Hey, this is getting easy!

A partial view of the resulting report is shown in Figure 20 below.

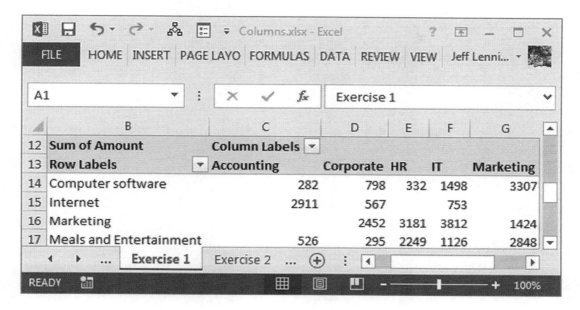

Figure 20

Our PivotTable summarizes the data as needed, and we have achieved the desired report.

EXERCISE 2—HEADERS

Now let's create the same report but clean up the headers.

 **PRACTICE**

To work along, please refer to the Exercise 2 worksheet.

The report in Figure 20 contains some funky report headers, namely Sum of Amount in *B12*, Column Labels in *C12*, and Row Labels in *B13*. Let's clean up our report by changing these funky headers.

We begin by building the following report from the data on the *Data* sheet:

- PT ROWS: Account; COLUMNS: Department; VALUES: Sum(Amount)

As previously discussed, there are several ways to change report labels. Because typing the new label into the cell is fast, we type Department Report into *B12*, Department into *C12*, and Account in *B13*. The cleaner version of our report is shown in Figure 21 below.

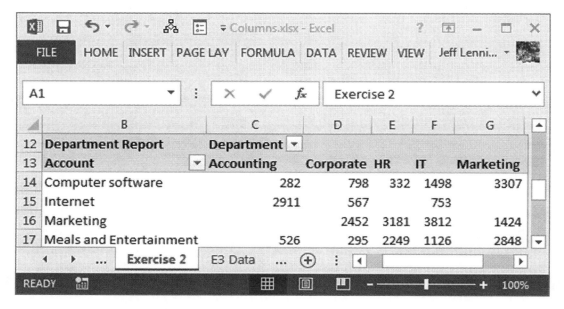

Figure 21

These header changes make our report easier to read and understand.

EXERCISE 3—STORES

In this exercise, we'll use a column field to transpose the data.

 **PRACTICE**

> To work along, please refer to the Exercise 3 worksheet.

We exported a transaction summary for the month and saved it on the *E3 Data* sheet. The extract includes Month, Item, Store, and Amount columns. Rather than view the summary in a vertical layout with all stores in a single column, we'd prefer to see the stores in a horizontal layout with each store in its own column. We can essentially transpose the summary from a vertical to a horizontal orientation by building the following report:

- PT ROWS: Item; COLUMNS: Store; VALUES: Sum(Amount)

We finish our report by cleaning up the report headers. We change Sum of Amount to Monthly Report, Column Labels to Store, and Row Labels to Item. Ah, yes, much better.

CHAPTER CONCLUSION

Column fields enable us to easily generate crosstab-style reports where each column reflects a subgroup of the population.

Chapter 7: Filter Fields

SET UP

So far we have discussed three of the four report layout areas. We have created row, value, and column fields. Now it is time to discuss report filter fields.

Filter fields create report filters that allow us to limit which data rows the report displays. For example, we could display a desired department, account, or region. The ability to report on a subset of the data provides several benefits and is a big deal. Without this ability, we would need to export only the specific transactions we wanted to include in the report. If we ever wanted to report on a different subset, we would need to generate another extract.

Additionally, filter fields allow us to use a single data source to feed multiple reports and subsequently apply filters as needed for each report. Last, report filters enable the data source to include all of the transactions that total an expected amount, helping us ensure our workbook is accurate and internally consistent. For example, the data source could include all transactions for the year, the total of which ties out to the expected amount, even though the report only includes transactions for a selected month. There are several ways to filter PivotTables. In this chapter, we explore report filters.

 XREF

Additional filter tools, such as field filter controls and slicers, are discussed in Chapter 19: Filtering.

HOW TO

To create a report filter field, simply insert the desired field into the filters area. For example, if we want to filter a report by department, we insert the department field into the filters area, as shown in Figure 22 below.

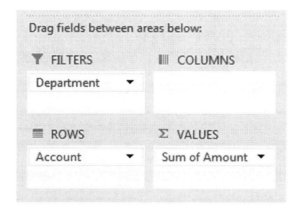

Figure 22

Using our convention, the report would be described as follows:

- PT ROWS: Account; VALUES: Sum(Amount); FILTERS: Department

The report filter is presented above the existing PivotTable, as illustrated by range ***B11:C11*** in Figure 23 below.

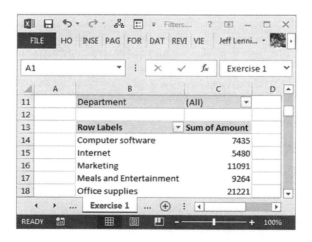

Figure 23

The interactive filter control shown in *C11* makes it easy to apply report filters. Initially all items are included, but you can select a specific department from the drop-down list.

NOTE

You can choose more than one item after checking the Select Multiple Items checkbox in the drop-down. The report values reflect the sum of all selected items.

You can create multiple report filters by inserting additional fields into the filters area.

EXAMPLES

Let's set up a few report filters to get the hang of it.

**PRACTICE**

To work along, please refer to *Filter Fields.xlsx*.

VIDEO

To watch the solutions video, please visit the Excel University Video Library.

EXERCISE 1—SINGLE FILTER

In this exercise, we'll make it easy to display any selected department.

**PRACTICE**

To work along, please refer to the Exercise 1 worksheet.

Our exported accounting data is stored on the *E1 Data* sheet. It contains TransID, AcctNum, Account, DeptNum, Department, Date, and Amount columns. Our report should summarize the transactions by account and make it easy to pick a department, so we set out to build the following report:

- PT ROWS: Account; VALUES: Sum(Amount); FILTERS: Department

In a new PivotTable, we insert the account field into the rows area, the amount field into the values area, and the department field into the filters area. The resulting report looks like the one shown in Figure 23. When we select a department from the drop-down, the report updates accordingly.

EXERCISE 2—MULTIPLE FILTERS

In this exercise, we'll use multiple report filters.

 **PRACTICE**

To work along, please refer to the Exercise 2 worksheet.

Our exported sales data is stored on the *E2 Data* sheet. The extract includes columns for Item, Region, Rep, and Amount. We would like to view a report by item and be able to select various combinations of reps and regions. We'll insert both the region and rep fields into the filters area and build the following report:

- PT ROWS: Item; VALUES: Sum(Amount); FILTERS: Region, Rep

In a new PivotTable, we insert the item field into the rows area, the amount field into the values area, and the region and rep fields into the filters area. In the resulting report, it is easy to pick and choose any combination of region and rep.

CHAPTER CONCLUSION

Since we have the ability to easily filter a report, we can quickly view different subsets of data. Additionally, the data source can include more transactions than needed to ensure it ties out to the expected total.

Chapter 8: Updating Data

SET UP

Let's take a moment and reflect on the PivotTable feature. It creates a report that summarizes a data source range. The report is separate from the data and typically resides on a different worksheet. We previously discussed the benefits of splitting data from reports, especially in recurring-use workbooks. One advantage is that we can easily update the report by pasting transactions into the data sheet.

 XREF

Splitting data from reports is discussed in Volume 1, Chapter 16.

By design, the PivotTable feature creates a report that is separate from the data. Once we've defined the report structure, we don't need to define it again. For example, during the next reporting period, we just paste updated data into the data sheet and refresh the report. I already sense your anxiety. I know; I feel it too. We are concerned that if the updated data contains more rows than the original data source, the additional rows will be improperly excluded from the report. We need to address this issue and others when updating PivotTable data. Let's work through the mechanics now.

HOW TO

We need to explore the following details related to PivotTable data:

- Cache

- Independent PivotTables

- Change Data Source

- Tables

- Active cell

- Dynamic report size

Let's start with the PivotTable cache.

CACHE

When you create the first PivotTable from a specific data source, Excel makes a static copy of the data and stores it in a PivotTable cache. The data flows into the cache and then to the PivotTable. Excel doesn't automatically refresh the cache when a user updates data source values. For example, if you change a cell value from 100 to 200, you won't find the updated amount in the PivotTable ... until you refresh the PivotTable cache.

There are several ways to refresh the PivotTable cache. If you are a right-clicker, right-click any PivotTable cell and select Refresh. If you prefer the Ribbon, use the following icon:

- PivotTable Tools > Analyze > Refresh

You'll notice that the Refresh Ribbon icon is split. Clicking the top refreshes the active PivotTable. Clicking the bottom expands a shortcut menu that includes additional refresh options, such as refreshing all PivotTables in the workbook.

If you prefer keyboard commands, use Alt+D, R (data, refresh) while the PivotTable is active.

INDEPENDENT PIVOTTABLES

A single data source can feed multiple PivotTables. Because PivotTables created from the same data source automatically share the same cache, when you refresh one, all are updated. Certain customizations are shared as well, such as calculated fields and custom grouping.

XREF

Grouping is discussed in Chapter 9: Groups and Subtotals. Calculated fields are discussed in Chapter 15: Calculated Fields.

In Excel versions prior to 2007, the PivotTable wizard provides the option to create independent PivotTables. Since independent PivotTables have their own cache, any change you make to one won't impact the others. Starting with Excel version 2007, this option is not presented, and Excel automatically sets up a shared cache to reduce file size and improve performance. However, you can open the legacy wizard to create independent PivotTables when needed by using the keyboard command below.

KB

To launch the legacy PivotTable wizard, which enables you to create independent PivotTables, use Alt+D, P (Data, PivotTable). Immediately finishing the wizard automatically creates independent PivotTables.

CHANGE DATA SOURCE

When you create a PivotTable from a worksheet range, the range reference is stored. When you refresh the report, Excel updates the report based on the values stored within that original range. Any values entered or pasted into cells outside of the original range are excluded from the report. Fortunately, it is pretty easy to expand the data source range to include new values. You can resize the dimensions of the data range or otherwise change the data source with the following Ribbon icon:

- PivotTable Tools > Analyze > Change Data Source

The resulting dialog box allows you to change the data source dimensions as needed. You can use standard keyboard shortcuts to select the range. For example, use Ctrl+Shift+Down Arrow to instantly extend the selection to the end of the data region.

Even though the change data source command is quick, it is a manual step. As you know, we seek to eliminate manual steps from our recurring-use workbooks. So rather than store the data in an ordinary worksheet range, we'll store it in a table.

TABLES

Since tables auto-expand to include new data rows and columns, they are a great place to store PivotTable data. Simply use the table's name as the data source. Storing data in a table ensures new rows and columns are included in the PivotTable when refreshed.

 NOTE

Although my personal preference is to use tables, another option to ensure new data rows are included is to define the data source with column-only references, such as *A:D*. Be advised that this approach may result in unexpected behavior, such as the inability to group date values. Additionally, when the data source range includes blank cells, the PivotTable may include the report label (blank). The (blank) label may be renamed or filtered out if needed.

 XREF

Renaming row labels is discussed in Chapter 18: Sorting. Filtering is discussed in Chapter 19: Filtering.

If you create the PivotTable before converting the data range to a table, you'll need to change the PivotTable's data source to the table's name. If you create the PivotTable after converting the data range to a table, Excel should automatically use the table's name, assuming the active cell lies within the table.

ACTIVE CELL

When you create a PivotTable, Excel needs to know two pieces of information: the data source and the report location. This information is requested in the Create PivotTable dialog box, shown in Figure 24 below.

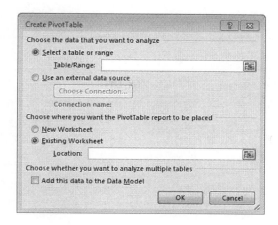

Figure 24

At the moment you open the dialog, Excel considers the active cell when populating the dialog fields. If the active cell is blank, Excel assumes it represents the location of the report and populates the existing worksheet location field accordingly. If the active cell is not blank, Excel assumes it represents the location of the data source and populates the dialog with the table name or range reference accordingly. Of course, you can always change these dialog values if Excel makes an incorrect assumption.

DYNAMIC REPORT SIZE

PivotTable reports dynamically change sizes to accommodate data updates. For example, you've created a report that includes three rows, one for each region in the data source. When you update the data next period, a fourth region appears in the transactions. When you refresh the report to include the new transactions, it dynamically expands to present all four regions. The report summarizes the transactions in the data source range and adjusts its dimensions as needed. This is fairly spectacular, and we'll explore the benefits of this special property when we compare report types.

XREF

Report type comparison is discussed in Chapter 11: Report Type Comparison.

All right, enough talk. Let's get busy with the exercises.

EXAMPLES

Let's update the data in several PivotTable reports.

 **PRACTICE**

To work along, please refer to *Updating Data.xlsx.*

 VIDEO

To watch the solutions video, please visit the Excel University Video Library.

EXERCISE 1—REFRESH

In this exercise, we'll update data source values and refresh a PivotTable.

PRACTICE

To work along, please refer to the Exercise 1 worksheet.

The data for our report is in an ordinary range stored on the **E1 Data** sheet. The extract contains TransID, Account, Date, and Amount columns. We would like to summarize the transactions by account, so we build the following report:

- PT ROWS: Account; VALUES: Sum(Amount)

We make a note of the report total: $38,512. We now change the amount of transaction 1985 from $264 to $300. When we flip back to the report, we notice that the total did not change. This is because the cache is outdated and needs to be refreshed. After we refresh the PivotTable using any of the techniques discussed above, we notice the report total has been updated to $38,548 as expected.

EXERCISE 2—CHANGE DATA SOURCE

In this exercise, we'll add a new record to the data source.

 **PRACTICE**

To work along, please refer to the Exercise 2 worksheet.

We export some data from our accounting system and store it in an ordinary range on the *E2 Data* sheet. The extract contains TransID, ItemNum, Date, and Amount columns. We'd like to summarize the transactions by item, so we build the following report:

- PT ROWS: ItemNum; VALUES: Sum(Amount)

We make a note of the report total. Now, back on the *E2 Data* sheet, we'll simulate adding a new transaction simply by copying the final transaction and pasting it under the range. Flipping back to the report, we notice the total is unchanged. Since we haven't refreshed the report yet, we expect this. When we refresh the report, we notice that the total remains unchanged.

The report excludes the new transaction because it lies outside of the original data source range. Fortunately, this is easy to change. We click the Change Data Source button on the Ribbon and use our keyboard or mouse to expand the selection to include the new data. Now when we look at the report total, we note it includes the new transaction.

EXERCISE 3—TABLE

In this exercise, we'll store the data in a table.

 **PRACTICE**

To work along, please refer to the Exercise 3 worksheet.

We export transactions from our accounting system, paste them into the *E3 Data* worksheet, convert the ordinary range into a table, and name the table *tbl_e3_data*. The table includes TransID, ItemNum, Date, and Amount columns. We would like to summarize the transactions by item, so using the table's name as the data source, we build the following report:

- PT ROWS: ItemNum; VALUES: Sum(Amount)

We make a note of the report total and get ready for the big test. We'll once again simulate adding a new transaction by copying the final transaction and pasting it immediately under the table. We note that the table auto-expands to include this new data row. Goose bumps! We refresh the report, and yes, the total updates to include the new item! Going forward, we'll plan to store our report data in tables.

CHAPTER CONCLUSION

In this chapter, we explored several details about PivotTable data and how to manage updates. We examined how data flows from the source to the cache and then to the report. We also discovered that tables are a great place to store source data.

Chapter 9: Groups and Subtotals

SET UP

The PivotTable feature supports groups and subtotals. Since they are closely related, we'll discuss both in this chapter. A group is a collection of row or column labels, such as all of the reps in a specific region. A report subtotal is generated by applying an aggregate function to the group's values, such as summing the sales for the region. Let's examine several options for creating groups and subtotals.

HOW TO

For our purposes, PivotTables support two types of groups: field groups and custom groups created with the group command. Report subtotals are available for both types of groups. Let's review field groups, custom groups, and subtotal options.

FIELD GROUPS

A field group is defined by the values in a data source column. For example, if our data included a region column, we could use it to create a group of row or column labels. Consider the following report:

- PT ROWS: Region, Rep; VALUES: Sum(Amount)

The report values are created by the rep field, and the report subtotals are created by the region field, as shown in Figure 25 below.

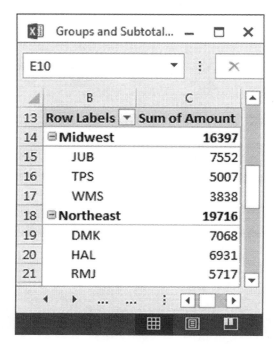

Figure 25

 NOTE

Each transaction for a given region is included in the region group, independent of the rep. If a rep has transactions for multiple regions, then the rep will be listed within multiple region groups.

When the desired report groups are defined within the data source, we can easily insert them into the report. When they are not, we can use the grouping command to create custom groups.

 XREF

We can also define a field group by creating a calculated field in the data source range, as discussed in Chapter 24: Data Preparation.

CUSTOM GROUPS

Using the group command, we are able to create custom groups of row and column labels. We'll explore the following:

- Date groups
- Manual groups
- Value groups

I've personally found the most benefit from date groups, so we'll start there.

Date Groups

Let's say our source data has a column with the date of each transaction. When we try to build a monthly report from the data, we quickly realize that we have no column that defines the group; that is, we have no month column. All we have is a date column. When we insert the date field into the rows area, we get one row for each transaction date. Since we want to view the report by month, not by date, we'll group the date field by month.

It's easy to group a date field. After inserting the date field into the report, select any of the date cells in the report. Open the Grouping dialog box either by right-clicking a date cell and selecting Group, or by using the following command icon:

- PivotTable Tools > Analyze > Group Selection

Excel realizes you are trying to group a date field and displays the relevant Grouping dialog box, shown in Figure 26 below.

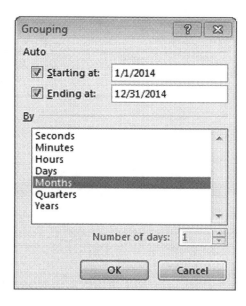

Figure 26

Accept the default selection of months by clicking OK. The report is now grouped by month. Pretty neat!

 NOTE

The number of days field in the dialog is enabled when you group by days and allows you to specify the number of days in each group.

NOTE

To group a date field, each cell within the data column needs to contain a date value. If you receive an error message, review the data source range to ensure it doesn't include blank rows and that all field cells contain a valid date.

You can pick several group options at once, such as year and month. This will group the report by year, and within each year, by month. This is a handy combination, because if you group only by month, all transactions for a month are included in the column, regardless of year. For example, all January transactions for all years in the data source will be included in a single January column. By selecting both years and months, you ensure that Excel creates a January column for each year.

XREF

When grouping date fields, Excel defaults to calendar year periods. To my knowledge, Excel does not have an option to change to fiscal year periods. Fiscal year field groups are discussed in Chapter 24: Data Preparation.

 NOTE

You can group a row or column date field, and once grouped, you can move it as needed, such as to the filters layout area.

Manual Groups

You can define manual groups by selecting the desired row or column labels and clicking the group command icon. Manual groups can be renamed as needed.

Value Groups

If a row or column field is numeric, you can group the field to create ranges such as 1–1,000, 1,001–2,000, and so on.

SUBTOTAL OPTIONS

Report subtotals generally sum the report values in each report group. We can turn subtotals on or off for any group, and select the function, such as sum, count, or average, by using the Field Settings dialog.

You can open the settings dialog for a specific field by right-clicking a related row or column label cell and selecting Field Settings from the shortcut menu, by clicking the field control in the report layout area and then Field Settings from the shortcut menu, or by selecting a row or column label cell for the desired field and then the following Ribbon command:

- PivotTable Tools > Analyze > Field Settings

Use the dialog to define one or more functions for the desired field. For example, to turn off subtotals for the Region field, select None, as shown in Figure 27 below.

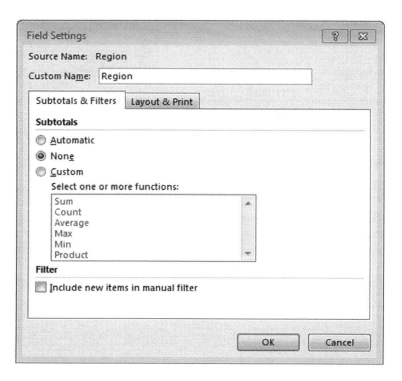

Figure 27

In addition to the Subtotals & Filters tab, the Layout & Print tab provides additional settings and options. Please feel free to investigate them and use the built-in Excel help system for additional information.

 NOTE

> The Field Settings dialog box is similar to the Value Field Setting dialog box explored previously, except that it contains options relevant for row and column fields rather than value fields.

If you just want to turn subtotals on or off, Excel provides a right-click shortcut and several related options under the following Ribbon icon:

- PivotTable Tools > Design > Subtotals

All right, let's crack open the exercises to practice.

EXAMPLES

We'll experiment with groups and subtotals in the following exercises.

 **PRACTICE**

To work along, please refer to *Groups and Subtotals.xlsx.*

 VIDEO

To watch the solutions video, please visit the Excel University Video Library.

EXERCISE 1—REMOVE REGION SUBTOTALS

In this exercise, we'll create a field group and remove subtotals.

 **PRACTICE**

To work along, please refer to the Exercise 1 worksheet.

We export sales transactions from our accounting system and store them in the *tbl_data* table on the *Data* sheet. The extract contains TransID, Region, Rep, Item, Date, and Amount columns. We want to view sales by rep and then group the reps by region. Since the group is defined by a data column, this task is really easy. We build the following report:

- PT ROWS: Region, Rep; VALUES: Sum(Amount)

We easily create this report. By default, Excel displays region subtotals, as shown in Figure 28 below.

Row Labels ▼	Sum of Amount
⊟ **Midwest**	**16397**
JUB	7552
TPS	5007
WMS	3838
⊟ **Northeast**	**19716**
DMK	7068
HAL	6931
RMJ	5717

Figure 28

Since we simply want to group the reps by region and are not concerned with the region subtotals, we decide to remove them. We turn off subtotals for the region row field using any of the techniques discussed previously, such as by right-clicking the Midwest label cell and unchecking the Subtotal shortcut item.

 NOTE

Turning off subtotals for the rep field instead of the region field will appear to have no effect on the PivotTable. This is because in the current layout the rep field represents the report values, not report subtotals. If you were to change the row field order to rep first and then region, then the rep amounts would represent report subtotals, and the report would reflect the subtotal setting accordingly.

The resulting report is shown in Figure 29 below.

Row Labels ▼	Sum of Amount
⊟ Midwest	
JUB	7552
TPS	5007
WMS	3838
⊟ Northeast	
DMK	7068
HAL	6931
RMJ	5717

Figure 29

 NOTE

If you hide the rep details by collapsing the region field, you will see region totals since they become the report values rather than the subtotal of report values.

 XREF

Displaying subtotals below the data is discussed in Chapter 13: Report Layout and Design.

EXERCISE 2—MONTH GROUPS

In this exercise, we'll group a date field by month.

 **PRACTICE**

To work along, please refer to the Exercise 2 worksheet.

Using the data from the previous exercise, we want to build a sales report with monthly columns. We decide to build the following report:

- PT ROWS: Rep; COLUMNS: Month; VALUES: Sum(Amount)

We easily insert the rep row field, but we get stuck when we try to insert the month column field because there is no month field. We'll need to group the date field by month, so we build the following report:

- PT ROWS: Rep; COLUMNS: Date; VALUES: Sum(Amount)

This report includes a column for each date. However, we want one column for each month, so we need to group the date field by month. This report is described with our report convention, as follows:

- PT ROWS: Rep; COLUMNS: Month(Date); VALUES: Sum(Amount)

We right-click any date cell and select Group from the shortcut menu. From the Grouping dialog, we select Months and click OK. Bam … the report has monthly columns! And the crowd goes wild! The resulting report is shown in Figure 30 below.

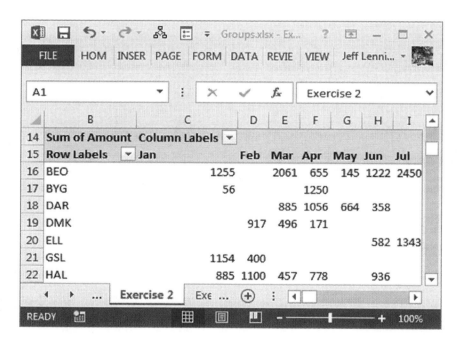

Figure 30

We have finished our report and life is good … or is it? Here is a question for you: if the underlying data spanned multiple years, how would our report present the data? I'll give you two choices. Would it place all January transactions, regardless of year, into a single January column? Or would it break out the years so that each year has its own January column? What do you think?

The answer is that it would place all January transactions, regardless of year, into a single January column. In fact, our data spanned multiple years, so please take a moment to verify this behavior. Since we typically prefer to see separate monthly columns for each year, the next exercise demonstrates how to group by month and year.

EXERCISE 3—MONTH AND YEAR GROUPS

In this exercise, we'll define both month and year groups.

 **PRACTICE**

To work along, please refer to the Exercise 3 worksheet.

Grouping a date field by month alone creates one column for each month, regardless of year. Fortunately, it is easy to break each year into a set of monthly columns. Using the data from the previous exercise, we build the following report:

- PT ROWS: Rep; COLUMNS: Month(Date); VALUES: Sum(Amount)

Did you notice that when you inserted the date field into the columns area, the date field was already grouped by month? Recall that PivotTables based on the same data source share the same cache. Since they are essentially linked, certain changes made to one, such as grouping a date field by month, flow to the others.

 XREF

The data cache is discussed in Chapter 8: Updating Data.

The final step in our report is to group the date field by both years and months. From the Grouping dialog, select both Years and Months. Now each year has its own set of monthly columns ... much better. It is a good habit to also group by years when you group by months.

Before we move to the next exercise, please note that our report now includes date and year column fields. The date field represents the month group, and the year field represents the year group. This allows us to independently define the location and settings for each. Currently the report is organized by year, and within each year, by month. This is because field order matters, and the year field is above the month field. If we want to see the report organized by month, and within each month by year, so that, for example, the January columns of the current and prior year are next to each other, then we can simply reorder the column fields so that the month field is above the year field. After defining the year group, we can reposition it as needed, even to other layout areas.

 NOTE

Now that our report includes a year group, go back to the previous exercise sheet and see if it also includes a year group. You can easily hide it by unchecking the field's checkbox.

Got time for one more exercise? Good.

EXERCISE 4—QUARTER GROUPS

In this exercise, we'll generate quarter groups and turn on quarter subtotals.

 **PRACTICE**

To work along, please refer to the Exercise 4 worksheet.

We want to build a report with year, quarter, and month groups. Using the data from the previous exercise, we create the following report:

- PT ROWS: Rep; COLUMNS: Year(Date), Quarter(Date), Month(Date); VALUES: Sum(Amount)

We easily group the date field by years, quarters, and months. But wait. Upon closer inspection, we notice that the quarter subtotals aren't displayed, even though they are displayed when we collapse or hide the monthly detail. It is odd that by default the only way to view quarter subtotals is by hiding the monthly detail.

So, can we display quarter subtotals and monthly values at the same time? Yes! We simply turn on subtotals for the quarter field using either the settings dialog box or the right-click shortcut menu. Now the PivotTable reflects the monthly columns and quarter subtotal columns.

CHAPTER CONCLUSION

Understanding how to group and display subtotals allows us to get our reports set up just right.

Chapter 10: Value Formats

SET UP

Have you noticed that in all of the reports we've created so far, the formatting of the value field was not inherited from the data source? For example, when a data source column was formatted as a currency, the report values were displayed without formatting. Like many other things in Excel, PivotTables operate on the stored values, not the displayed values. This chapter shows how to format value fields.

When you go to format PivotTable values, every instinct tells you to format the worksheet cells. After all, this is how you have formatted every number in every workbook your whole life. But your instinct would be wrong. And if your instinct is wrong, then the opposite would have to be right. You Seinfeld fans know what I'm talking about.

The issue is that the dimensions of a PivotTable might change over time. For example, when we insert a new row field or update the data, the cells that store report values change. As such, formatting worksheet cells is not an effective long-term approach. Although Excel attempts to update cell formats as the report dimensions change, it is a good habit to define the value formats within the PivotTable instead. Fortunately, this is easy to do.

HOW TO

To format PivotTable values, you want to format the field, not the worksheet cells. To format a value field, simply open the Value Field Settings dialog box and then click the Number Format button, as shown in Figure 31 below.

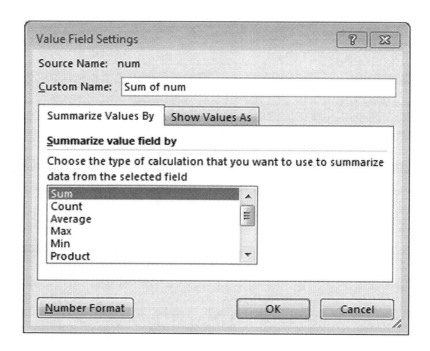

Figure 31

Clicking the Number Format button opens the Format Cells dialog box, which allows you to specify the desired format for the field. Although the dialog box is named Format Cells, it is slightly different from the standard Format Cells dialog box because it includes the Number tab only and excludes other tabs such as Alignment, Font, and Border.

Another way to open the dialog box is to right-click any value cell and select Number Format from the shortcut menu. Notice that the shortcut menu includes both Number Format and Format Cells. You need to select Number Format, since it will apply the formatting to the field rather than the cell.

EXAMPLES

Now let's practice formatting value fields rather than worksheet cells.

 **PRACTICE**

To work along, please refer to **Value Formats.xlsx.**

 VIDEO

To watch the solutions video, please visit the Excel University Video Library.

EXERCISE 1—NUMBER FORMAT

In this exercise, we'll apply a simple number format.

 **PRACTICE**

To work along, please refer to the Exercise 1 worksheet.

The exported transactions are stored in the **tbl_data** table on the **Data** sheet. The extract contains CkNum, VID, Vendor, AcctNum, Account, Date, and Amount columns. Since we want to view a summary by vendor ID, we build the following report:

- PT ROWS: VID; VALUES: Sum(Amount)

We want to format the value field, so we open the Value Field Settings dialog and then click the Number Format button. In the Format Cells dialog box, we format the field as a number and use the thousands comma separator and zero decimal places. The resulting report is much easier to read.

The best part is that this format is applied to all report values, even when the dimensions of the report change. For example, modify the report

- PT ROWS: Account, VID; VALUES: Sum(Amount)

Even though the report is now taller, all values adopt the desired formatting. That is the beauty of formatting the field rather than the worksheet cells.

EXERCISE 2—CURRENCY FORMAT

In this exercise, we'll apply a currency format.

 **PRACTICE**

To work along, please refer to the Exercise 2 worksheet.

We want to summarize the data from the previous exercise by account, so we build the following report:

* PT ROWS: Account; VALUES: Sum(Amount)

This time, rather than open the Value Field Settings dialog, we simply right-click any value cell and select Number Format. In the Format Cells dialog, we format the field as a currency with the $ symbol, comma thousands separator, and no decimal places. We confirm that we successfully formatted the field, and not just the right-clicked cell, since we can see all report values are formatted as desired.

CHAPTER CONCLUSION

Formatting value fields rather than worksheet cells will improve efficiency and enhance the readability of our reports.

Chapter 11: Report Type Comparison

SET UP

At this point we have a working knowledge of PivotTables. Before examining more details in the next section, we'll take a break to compare report types. We are exploring PivotTable reports in this volume, and we created many formula-based reports in Volume 2. Each type of report has advantages and disadvantages, and we need to consider the objectives, workbook, and report requirements before determining which to use. Let's review the key differences to make selecting the most appropriate report type easier.

Table 1 summarizes the differences we'll address in detail.

Item	Formula-Based Reports	PivotTable Reports
Prepare	Write formulas	PivotTable interface
Structure	Formula limits	Limited to layout options
Interactivity	Excel features (sort, filter)	Drill-down, sort, filter
Refresh Data	Automatic	Refresh button
New Items in Data	Manually add to report	Automatically included
Update Sort	Manual	Automatic
Labels without Data	Included	Excluded
Data	Structured and unstructured	Structured only

Table 1

Prepare

Let's examine how we prepare each report. We build a formula-based report by creating the row and column labels and then writing formulas that summarize the amounts in the source data range. The report value cells contain formulas.

We build a PivotTable report by interacting with the PivotTable interface. For example, we identify row and value fields by dragging the fields into the appropriate layout areas. The report value cells contain stored values.

Structure

Formula-based reports have no structure limits imposed and can be designed with virtually any layout. For example, formula-based reports can include blank rows and columns, store subtotals in arbitrary locations, add and subtract values as needed, and retrieve values from multiple locations.

PivotTable reports, on the other hand, have limits imposed by the PivotTable feature. For example, we can only place fields into the four layout areas. Additionally, we can't easily insert blank rows and columns at will, add and subtract amounts as needed, or pull values from multiple locations.

 NOTE

The PowerPivot feature is able to use data from multiple locations. Please use the Excel help system for more information.

Here is a question for you: which report type is more appropriate for building complex financial statements? Yes, probably a formula-based report.

Interactivity

Formula-based reports aren't very interactive and don't easily allow you to modify the report structure or drill into the details of a number. You can use certain Excel features such as basic sorting and filtering, but at the risk of breaking the formulas. For our purposes, we'll think about formula reports as having limited, if any, interactivity.

PivotTable reports are alive and fully interactive. A user can easily change the sort order, apply a filter, transpose the labels, and drill into the detail of any amount.

Here's another question for you: which type of report is more appropriate for delivering interactive digital reports? Yes, probably a PivotTable.

Refresh Data

When we insert new transactions into the data source table, values in formula-based reports are instantly and automatically recalculated.

Since values in PivotTable reports are based on the cache, we need to refresh it to update the report values.

Here's yet another question: which type of report ensures the report displays all transactions in the data source? The answer is that it depends on whether there are any new report labels in the data. Let's see how each report type accommodates new data items.

New Items in Data

How formula-based and PivotTable reports handle new data items is one of the most exciting differences between the two types of reports. For example, let's say we append new transactions to the source table. Because the data is stored in a table, new transaction rows will be included in both report types without issue. Our focus is on how any new items, such as new accounts or regions, will be included in the report as new labels. For the following discussion, let's assume that we build a report to summarize the data by account and that the new transactions include a new account.

A formula-based report will ignore the new account and exclude related transactions. To include the transactions, we must manually add the new report label and fill the amount formula into the new report row.

A PivotTable report automatically displays the new report label, includes the related transactions, and expands its dimensions as needed. This is super cool and one of my favorite things about PivotTables.

Here's a question: which type of report is most appropriate when new items are frequently added? Exactly, a PivotTable. PivotTable reports summarize the data, whatever it may be, according to the defined structure.

 XREF

You can test that new items are included in the report by comparing the report total to the data total on an ErrorCk sheet, as discussed in Volume 2, Chapter 25.

Update Sort

In a formula-based report, if the underlying data changes and you need to update the sort order, you will need to manually sort it.

In a PivotTable report, you define the sort order once, and each time the report is refreshed, the order is updated accordingly. This is true whether you sort by row label or by report value.

Here's a question: when the sort order is important and the data changes frequently, which report type is appropriate? Yes, I agree, a PivotTable.

Labels without Data

Formula-based reports typically have static report labels and formulas that retrieve related transactions. Report labels are displayed in the report even when there are no related transactions.

PivotTable reports summarize the data, whatever it may be, according to the defined structure. If there are no transactions for an item, it will not appear in the PivotTable.

Here's a question: if you need a report to display all accounts, even though selected accounts have no related transactions, which type is most appropriate? Yep, a formula-based report.

Data

While both formula-based reports and PivotTables operate best on flat data, formula-based reports are better able to adapt to unstructured data. We can use sophisticated functions and formulas to retrieve data from various layouts. For example, formula-based reports can use data even if the data includes blank columns, excludes column headers, or stores values and labels on different rows.

PivotTables have strict data requirements. For example, it must be flat, contain a header row, and can't have blank columns.

When the underlying data is stored in a crazy format, which report type is more appropriate? I agree, a formula-based report is probably a better fit.

HOW TO

To explore these differences, we'll build a formula-based report and a corresponding PivotTable version in each of the following exercises. This is going to be awesome!

Before we begin, let's take a look at the key PivotTable terms shown in Figure 32 below.

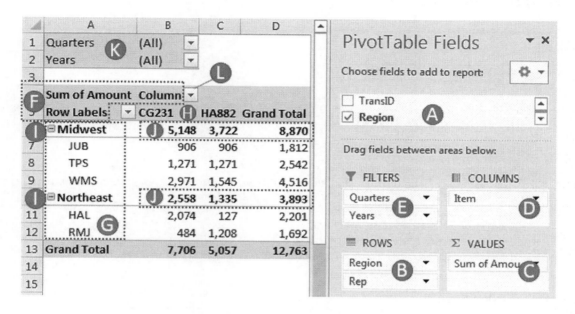

Figure 32

A. Field list

B. Row fields

C. Value fields

D. Column fields

E. Filter fields

F. Report headers

G. Row labels

H. Column labels

I. Groups

J. Subtotals

K. Report filters

L. Field filters

EXAMPLES

To compare report types, we'll build a formula-based report and then create the same report with the PivotTable feature. Please work along and complete the exercises below.

PRACTICE

To work along, please refer to **Report Type Comparison.xlsx**.

VIDEO

To watch the solutions video, please visit the Excel University Video Library.

NOTE

In Volumes 1 and 2, we discussed at length the features, functions, and techniques used to create formula-based reports. As such, I'm assuming that if I provide summary instructions, such as "Generate a unique list of report labels with the remove duplicates feature," and leave out the detailed steps, functions, and mechanics, you will be able to comfortably create formula-based reports throughout the remainder of this text.

EXERCISE 1—WARM-UP

In this exercise, we'll summarize the data by item.

PRACTICE

To work along, please refer to the Exercise 1 worksheet.

The data we exported from our accounting system is stored on the *E1 Data* sheet in the *tbl_e1_data* table. The data extract contains TransID, ItemNum, Date, and Amt columns.

Let's build the formula report using features, functions, and techniques discussed in previous volumes. We generate a unique list of ItemNum report labels with the remove duplicates feature. To populate the report values, we turn to our dear friend, SUMIFS.

Since the first report label is stored in *B11*, we write the following formula in *C11* and fill it down to populate the amount column:

```
=SUMIFS(tbl_e1_data[Amt],tbl_e1_data[ItemNum],B11)
```

Where:

- **tbl_e1_data[Amt]** is the column of numbers to add, the amount column

- **tbl_e1_data[ItemNum]** is the criteria range, the item number column

- **B11** is the criteria value, the item number

We finish the report by inserting a skinny row, creating a total with the SUBTOTAL function, and formatting the cells.

 XREF

The remove duplicates feature is discussed in Volume 2, Chapter 6. The skinny row technique is discussed in Volume 1, Chapter 12. The SUBTOTAL function is discussed in Volume 1, Chapter 11.

The resulting report is shown in Figure 33 below.

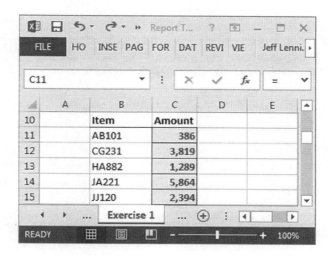

Figure 33

Now let's see if we can create the report with a PivotTable. We easily build the following report:

- PT ROWS: ItemNum; VALUES: Sum(Amount)

We finish the report by formatting the value field and changing the report headers from ItemNum, Sum of Amt, and Grand Total to Item, Amount, and Total, respectively. The resulting report is shown in Figure 34 below.

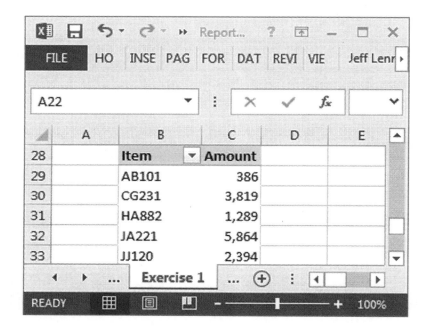

Figure 34

Wow, the two reports are really similar! They display the same amounts and have the same basic layout. Although there are minor cosmetic differences, such as the cell fill and the skinny row, they are essentially the same report. One was prepared with formulas and one with the PivotTable feature.

Was that fun? I hope so, because we are just getting warmed up, baby!

EXERCISE 2—CROSSTAB

In this exercise, we'll build a formula-based report with multiple columns and then reproduce it with a PivotTable.

 **PRACTICE**

To work along, please refer to the Exercise 2 worksheet.

The data extract has Item, Region, and Amount columns and is stored in the *tbl_e2_data* table on the *E2 Data* sheet. We want to summarize the data by item and include a column for each region.

Let's start with the formula-based report. We create and sort the report labels, compute the values with the SUMIFS function, and apply a few finishing touches such as adding the skinny row, formatting, and totals. The completed report is shown in Figure 35 below.

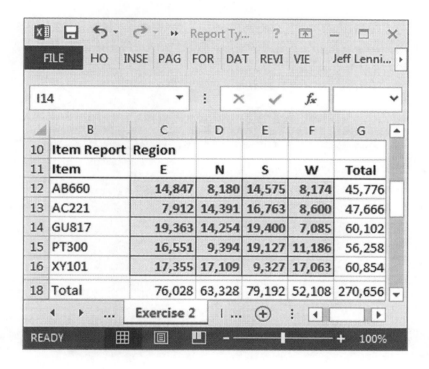

	B	C	D	E	F	G
10	**Item Report**	**Region**				
11	**Item**	**E**	**N**	**S**	**W**	**Total**
12	AB660	14,847	8,180	14,575	8,174	45,776
13	AC221	7,912	14,391	16,763	8,600	47,666
14	GU817	19,363	14,254	19,400	7,085	60,102
15	PT300	16,551	9,394	19,127	11,186	56,258
16	XY101	17,355	17,109	9,327	17,063	60,854
18	Total	76,028	63,328	79,192	52,108	270,656

Figure 35

Now, to create the PivotTable version, we simply build the following report:

• PT ROWS: Item; COLUMNS: Region; VALUES: Sum(Amount)

We finish by formatting the values and changing the default report headers to match our formula report. The resulting PivotTable is shown in Figure 36 below.

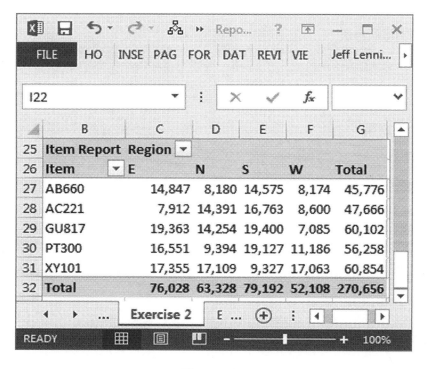

Figure 36

It is thrilling to reproduce our formula-based report with a PivotTable!

EXERCISE 3—NEW ITEMS

In this exercise, we'll see how both report types accommodate new items.

 **PRACTICE**

To work along, please refer to the Exercise 3 worksheet.

The exported general ledger data is stored in the *tbl_e3_data* table on the *E3 Data* sheet and contains TransID, AcctNum, Account, Date, and Amount columns. We want to summarize the data by account.

Let's begin with the formula report. We create and sort the account labels, compute the values with SUMIFS, add skinny and total rows, and splash on some cell formatting.

Next is the PivotTable version. We build the following report:

- PT ROWS: Account; VALUES: Sum(Amount)

We finish it with a few cosmetic touches, such as formatting the amount field and changing the report headers from Row Labels and Sum of Amount to Account and Amount, respectively.

 NOTE

When changing the report header from Sum of Amount to Amount, you may receive an error because the name conflicts with an existing field name. One common workaround is to add a trailing space to the end of the header.

Both reports are looking good. To see how they behave with new data, we add the following transaction to the data table:

- TransID = 2994

- AcctNum = 5101

- Account = Dues

- Date = 12/15/2015

- Amount = $1,500

Notice the transaction introduces a new account to the data table. Let's flip back to our reports and compare them. To add the new account to the formula-based report, we have to insert a new row, enter the account label, and fill the formula down. It is much faster to add the account to the PivotTable, since we simply click the Refresh button. Remarkable!

EXERCISE 4—LABELS WITHOUT DATA

In this exercise, we'll see how both types handle report labels without transactions in the data table.

 **PRACTICE**

To work along, please refer to the Exercise 4 worksheet.

The exported general ledger data is stored on the *E4 Data* sheet in the *tbl_e4_data* table and contains TransID, AcctNum, Account, Date, and Amount columns. We want to build a report that shows the totals for our accounts. The report needs to include all accounts, even those without any transactions.

Let's first build a formula-based report. We use the chart of accounts to create the labels, compute the values with SUMIFS, apply cell formatting, insert a skinny row, and add a total. The finished report is shown in Figure 37 below.

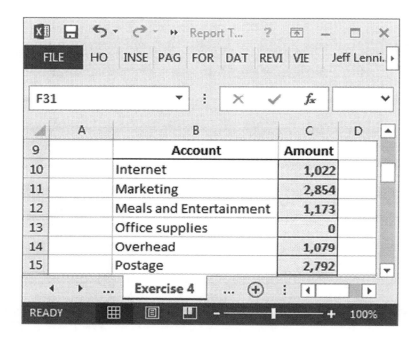

Figure 37

All accounts, even those without transactions, such as office supplies, are included in the report.

For the PivotTable version, we build the following report:

- PT ROWS: Account; VALUES: Sum(Amount)

We finish it by updating the headers and formatting the amount field. The resulting report is shown in Figure 38 below.

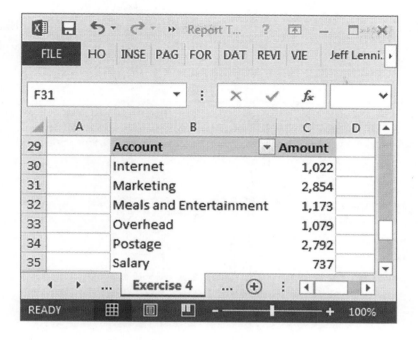

Figure 38

This report excludes accounts without transactions, such as office supplies. Since our report needs to include all accounts, even those without transactions, we'll use the formula-based version.

 NOTE

You can build a PivotTable report that includes labels for all accounts, even those without data, by pasting an account list into the data source with zero amounts. This essentially creates a transaction for each account.

EXERCISE 5—V2 REVISITED

I'm so excited about this exercise! I planned it as I was finishing Volume 2 and have been waiting anxiously to give it to you. I hope you like it!

 **PRACTICE**

To work along, please refer to the Exercise 5 worksheet.

In Volume 2's final exercise, we built a very cool formula-based report that allowed the user to filter by department and year. A copy of that report, which summarizes the data in the **tbl_e5_data** table stored on the **E5 Data** sheet, is shown in Figure 39 below.

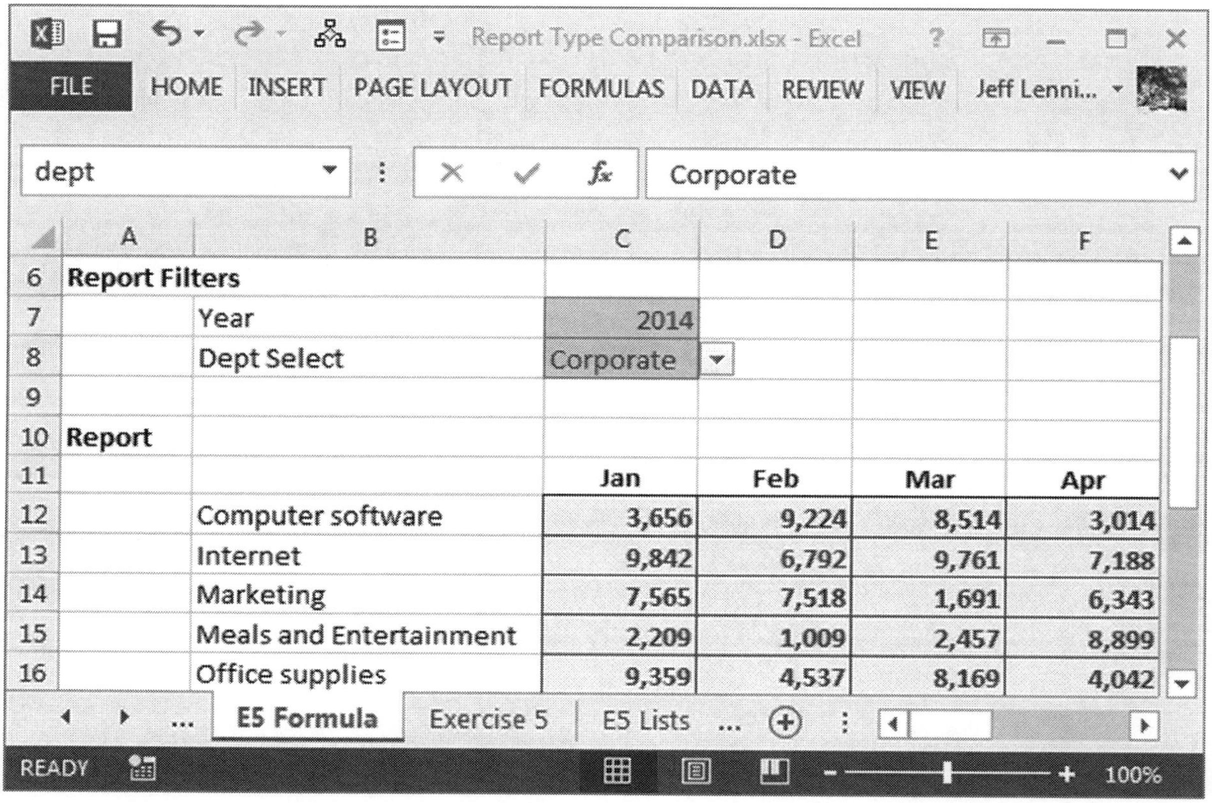

Figure 39

We used many features, functions, and techniques, and it took a while to build the report. We used the remove duplicates feature to generate the row labels, the EOMONTH function to create the dynamic column labels, the table feature to store the list of departments, the data validation feature to provide the department filter, the input cell style to highlight the filter cells, the skinny row technique, the SUBTOTAL function to compute the totals, and the SUMIFS function with concatenation to compute the values, as shown in the formula below:

```
=SUMIFS(tbl_e5_data[Amount],
tbl_e5_data[Dept],dept,
```

```
tbl_e5_data[Account],$B12,
tbl_e5_data[Date],">="&C$11,
tbl_e5_data[Date],"<="&EOMONTH(C$11,0))
```

Now we have all of the skills needed to create the same report without writing a single formula!

Let's break it down. We have one row for each account, one column for each month, and report filters for year and department. It sounds like the following PivotTable would work:

- PT ROWS: Account; COLUMNS: Month(Date); VALUES: Sum(Amount); FILTERS: Year(Date), Department

Could it be that easy? Can we really build this report in seconds rather than minutes? Yes! On your mark ... get set ... go. Wow, what a rush!

 NOTE

> To create a year filter, place the date field into the rows or columns area, group it by year, and then move the resulting year field to the filters area.

CHAPTER CONCLUSION

There are different ways to build reports in Excel. Knowing the differences between formula-based reports and PivotTable reports enables us to determine which report to use based on the objectives, workbook, and requirements. The next section continues to build our proficiency with PivotTables, which is good, because PivotTables help us use Excel like a boss.

WORKING WITH PIVOTTABLES

Pivot Tables help you use Excel like a boss.

Chapter 12: Options

SET UP

I'm not sure about you, but I had a great time in the last chapter getting PivotTable reports to look like formula-based reports. In this section, we'll continue that process, because it will surely help you feel comfortable converting existing formula-based reports to PivotTables when appropriate. Many of the exercises in this section ask you to first build a formula-based report and then try to reproduce it with a PivotTable.

Additionally, I have a couple of surprises that will strengthen your formula-based reports. Building on the content from previous volumes, this section demonstrates how to lock down table references and build dynamic SUMIFS functions.

 XREF

> Locking down table references and building dynamic SUMIFS functions are discussed in Chapter 14: Multiple Value Fields.

Let's begin by exploring various PivotTable options. Just as there are field settings, there are report settings. The report settings enable us to control various report elements.

HOW TO

The report settings are available in the PivotTable Options dialog, which you can open by right-clicking any cell in the report and selecting PivotTable Options or navigating to the following Ribbon command:

- PivotTable Tools > Analyze > Options

The PivotTable Options dialog is shown in Figure 40 below.

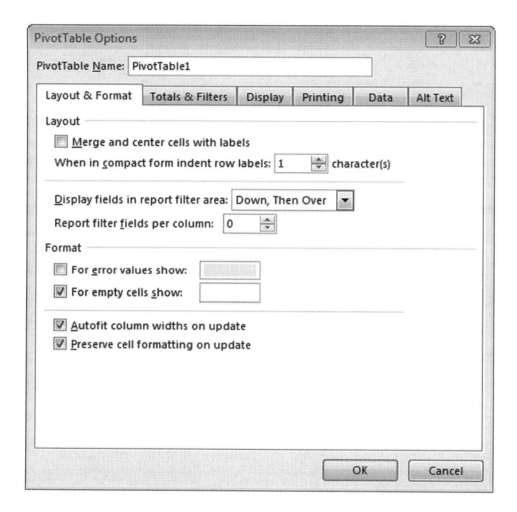

Figure 40

Here is a brief description of the options available on the various dialog tabs:

- Layout & Format—control how the report appears within the worksheet

- Totals & Filters—control the display of grand totals, sorting, and filters

- Display—control user interface options, such as display of the +/- buttons

- Printing—control how the report appears when printing to a printer or digital format

- Data—options related to the source data, such as disabling drill down, saving data with the file, and retaining deleted items

- Alt Text—describe the report content

Let's take a quick tour of my favorite options:

Layout & Format

- *For empty cells show*—blank by default, this option defines the stored value of empty cells. This is useful in crosstab-style reports when certain combinations of row and column labels have no transactions.

- *Autofit column widths on update*—checked by default, this option automatically changes column widths to accommodate the data. Uncheck it, and Excel will leave your column widths alone.

Totals & Filters

- *Show grand totals for rows*—checked by default, this option computes totals for each row and displays them in a grand total column.

- *Show grand totals for columns*—checked by default, this option computes totals for each column and displays them in a grand total row.

Display

- *Show expand/collapse buttons*—checked by default, this option controls the display of the little +/- buttons that show/hide group detail.

This is my short list of favorites, but please explore the many other available options to see if they are useful in your PivotTables.

EXAMPLES

Let's work on a few examples to get comfortable changing PivotTable options.

 **PRACTICE**

To work along, please refer to *Options.xlsx*.

VIDEO

To watch the solutions video, please visit the Excel University Video Library.

EXERCISE 1—EMPTY CELLS

The purpose of this exercise is to demonstrate how to control the display of empty cells.

**PRACTICE**

To work along, please refer to the Exercise 1 worksheet.

In this exercise, we'll use an option to get our PivotTable to look more like its formula-based counterpart. The exported data is stored on the **Data** sheet in the **tbl_data** table and contains TransID, Region, Rep, Item, Date, and Amount columns. We want a summary by item with region columns.

Starting with the formula report, we prepare the labels with the remove duplicates feature, generate the values with the SUMIFS function, and apply some basic formatting. We note that when a given combination of item and region has no transactions, the SUMIFS function returns zero.

XREF

When there are no matching items, SUMIFS returns 0, as discussed in Volume 2, Chapter 15.

For the PivotTable version, we build the following report:

- PT ROWS: Item; COLUMNS: Region; VALUES: Sum(Amount)

We update the report labels and format the value field. We note that when a given combination of item and region has no data, the report reflects an empty cell. This is different from our formula report, which displays zero instead of an empty cell. Since we want the PivotTable to closely resemble the formula report, we'll open the PivotTable Options dialog box and tell Excel to show zero for empty cells. The updated report is shown in Figure 41 below.

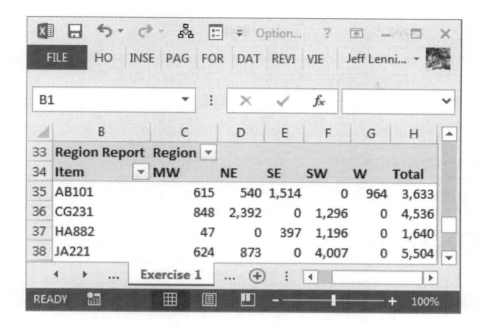

Figure 41

Ah, yes, now the PivotTable closely matches the formula-based report.

Before we move on, did you notice that when we build PivotTables, Excel messes with our column widths? Look at the exercise worksheet, and you'll see that column **B** is wider than **C**, which is wider than **D**, which is wider than **E**. Can we prevent Excel from changing our column widths? We can, and we will in the next exercise.

EXERCISE 2—COLUMN WIDTHS

In this exercise, we'll build the same report as the previous exercise, but this time we'll prevent Excel from changing column widths.

 **PRACTICE**

To work along, please refer to the Exercise 2 worksheet.

Although we can uncheck the autofit column widths option at any time, we'll uncheck it before inserting any fields to prevent Excel from resizing our existing columns. We begin by inserting a new PivotTable.

Next, we open the PivotTable Options dialog box and uncheck the autofit checkbox. Then we create the following report:

- PT ROWS: Item; COLUMNS: Region; VALUES: Sum(Amount)

We notice that the column widths remain unchanged, unlike the worksheet from the previous exercise.

EXERCISE 3—GRAND TOTAL

The purpose of this exercise is to demonstrate how to control the display of grand totals.

 **PRACTICE**

To work along, please refer to the Exercise 3 worksheet.

The exported data is stored on the *E3 Data* sheet in the *tbl_e3_data* table, and contains Dept, Date, Type, and Amount. The type column tells us if the row represents actual or budget data. We would like to create a report by department and include one column for budget and one for actual.

Let's start with the formula-based version, which will contain department, actual, and budget columns. We prepare the labels and use our trusty SUMIFS function to compute the values. We apply some basic formatting, and the report looks good.

We generate the PivotTable version as follows:

- PT ROWS: Dept; COLUMNS: Type; VALUES: Sum(Amount)

We update the headers and format the value field. The resulting report includes department, actual, budget, and total columns. The total column makes no sense. We don't want to add actual and budget values. We may want to compute the difference or variance, but certainly not the sum.

 XREF

We will compute the variance in Chapter 15: Calculated Fields.

Since we don't want to display the total column, we'll remove it either by opening the PivotTable Options dialog box and unchecking Show grand totals for rows or by selecting the following Ribbon command:

- PivotTable Tools > Design > Grand Totals > On for Columns Only

The resulting report is shown Figure 42 below.

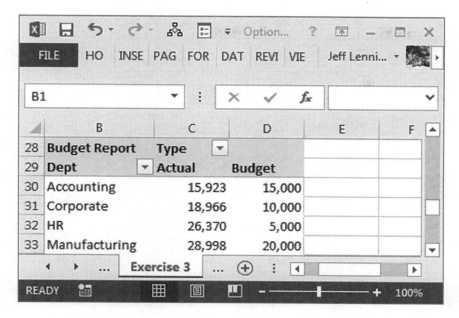

Figure 42

Much better! Now the PivotTable more closely matches our formula report.

CHAPTER CONCLUSION

This chapter covered the PivotTable options that I find most useful, but many additional settings are available. I encourage you to take a moment to explore them, because they may come in handy.

Chapter 13: Report Layout and Design

SET UP

PivotTables have different layout formats, and thus far we've only used one of them. Before we jump into the details, let's have a quick history lesson. Back in Excel version 2003 and prior, each row field got its own column. This had both pros and cons. It was easy to filter row fields, and the report was easy to read. The disadvantage was that value columns shifted when new row fields were inserted.

With version 2007, Microsoft incorporated the following layout options: compact, outline, and tabular. The default layout is compact, which essentially displays all row fields in a single column. Every PivotTable we've created so far has used this layout. Let's explore how to switch layouts.

HOW TO

There are a variety of report layout and design options available on the following Ribbon tab:

- PivotTable Tools > Design

Let's start with the Report Layout icon. Clicking it reveals several choices:

- Show in Compact Form—displays all row fields in a single column, and defaults to placing subtotals above the summarized data

- Show in Outline Form—displays each row field in its own column, and defaults to placing subtotals above the summarized data

- Show in Tabular Form—displays each row field in its own column, and places subtotals under the summarized data

- Repeat All Item Labels—repeats labels for grouped row and column fields

- Do Not Repeat Item Labels—does not repeat labels for grouped row and column fields

 NOTE

The repeat item labels options were first available in Excel 2010. The Repeat All Item Labels command repeats labels for all fields. To repeat labels for a specific field, open its settings dialog box and check the Repeat Item Labels checkbox on the Layout & Print tab.

The Subtotals icon lets you display subtotals above or below the summarized data, or turn them off altogether. You can show subtotals at the bottom of the group in compact, outline, and tabular layouts. You can show subtotals at the top of the group in compact and outline layouts.

The Grand Totals icon lets you control the display of report totals, and the Blank Rows icon lets you display a blank row after item groups.

Be sure to explore the colorful PivotTable styles and options, such as banded rows and columns.

 NOTE

You can create a custom PivotTable style by expanding the Styles list and selecting New PivotTable Style.

 NOTE

Using the following special selection technique, you can manually format a PivotTable. If you hover the mouse along the top border of the desired cell, the cursor changes to a down arrow. If you hover over the left cell border, the cursor turns into a right arrow. Click to select all related cells, such as all group labels or subtotals. Any formatting is applied to all selected and future items.

EXAMPLES

Let's play with a few layout and design options.

**PRACTICE**

To work along, please refer to *Report Layout.xlsx.*

VIDEO

To watch the solutions video, please visit the Excel University Video Library.

EXERCISE 1—ACCOUNTS

In this exercise, we'll use layout and design options to help our PivotTable resemble its formula-based counterpart.

**PRACTICE**

To work along, please refer to the Exercise 1 worksheet.

The exported data is stored on the *E1 Data* sheet in the *tbl_e1_data* table and contains TransID, AcctNum, Account, Date, and Amount columns. We'd like to see a summary by account.

We begin with the formula report. Since we want to display both account number and name, we generate two label columns. We use SUMIFS to compute the values and splash on some formatting. The resulting report is shown in Figure 43 below.

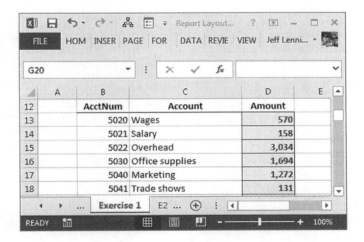

Figure 43

For the PivotTable version, we begin with the following:

- PT ROWS: AcctNum, Account; VALUES: Sum(Amount)

Excel applies the default layout, which places all row labels in a single column, as shown in Figure 44 below.

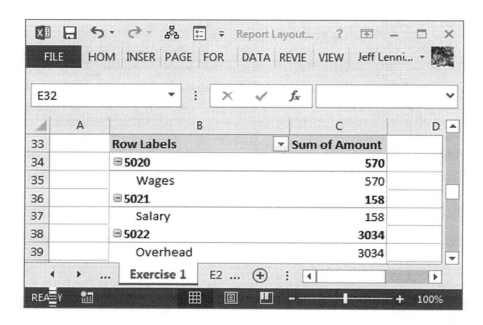

Figure 44

Although the PivotTable contains the same values as the formula report, the layout is much different. The formula report presents each account number and name on the same row in separate columns, but the PivotTable report displays them on different rows in the same column. To get the labels into separate columns, we change the PivotTable layout to tabular. The result is better, but still different, because each account displays a subtotal row that we don't want. Remember: field groups automatically generate subtotals.

XREF

Group subtotals are discussed in Chapter 9: Groups and Subtotals.

Since our report has two row fields, account number and account name, Excel automatically groups and subtotals the report by account number. We can turn off the subtotals by using the Field Settings dialog box or the following Ribbon command:

- PivotTable Tools > Design > Subtotals > Do Not Show Subtotals

Again the result is better, but still different. The PivotTable now has small +/- buttons in the account number cells that expand or collapse the field. We can easily hide the +/- buttons using the PivotTable Options dialog box or the following Ribbon command:

- PivotTable Tools > Analyze > +/- Buttons

The new look is much better. We finish by formatting the value field, and updating the column header from Sum of Amount to Amount (with a trailing space). Our resulting PivotTable, shown in Figure 45 below, closely resembles our formula report.

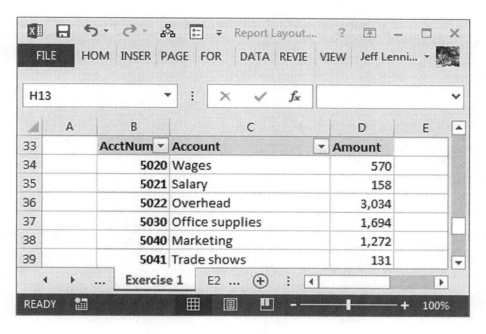

Figure 45

The time we spent getting the report dialed in will pay off in future periods. When we update the data and refresh the report, we know that unlike the formula report, any new accounts will be automatically included in our PivotTable.

EXERCISE 2—REGIONS

In this exercise, we'll repeat labels to reproduce a formula-based report.

 **PRACTICE**

To work along, please refer to the Exercise 2 worksheet.

The exported sales data is stored on the *E2 Data* sheet in the *tbl_e2_data* table, and contains TransID, Region, Rep, Item, Date, and Amount columns. We'd like to see a summary by region by rep.

Beginning with the formula report, we generate the labels, and include both region and rep columns. We use our dear friend SUMIFS to populate the amount column. We slap on some formatting and create a skinny and total row. The resulting report is shown in Figure 46.

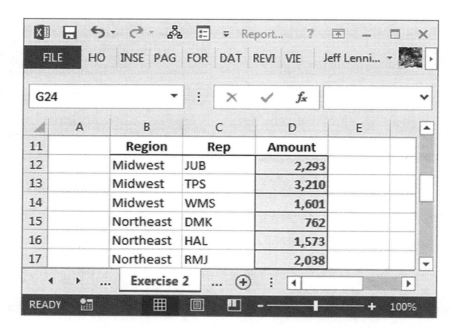

Figure 46

Easy enough. For the PivotTable version, we begin with the following:

- PT ROWS: Region, Rep; VALUES: Sum(Amount)

The resulting report is a good start, but we still have some work to do to simulate the formula version. After changing the layout from compact to tabular, we notice one main difference. Each region label is displayed once in the PivotTable and is repeated through all rows of the formula report. Fortunately, we can easily repeat row labels by using the following Ribbon command:

- PivotTable Tools > Design > Report Layout > Repeat All Item Labels

Bam, that is much better! We address a few remaining cosmetic differences by formatting the value field, updating the headers, hiding the +/- buttons, unchecking the row headers style option so the region column labels aren't bold, and removing region subtotals. The resulting report is shown in Figure 47 below.

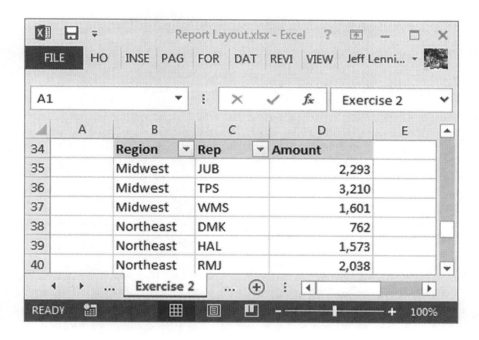

Figure 47

This PivotTable is a decent reproduction of the formula report.

EXERCISE 3—EMPLOYEES

In this exercise, we'll build PivotTable and formula-based versions of the same report.

PRACTICE

To work along, please refer to the Exercise 3 worksheet.

The exported payroll data is stored on the *E3 Data* sheet in the *tbl_e3_data* table and contains PayDate, FirstName, LastName, Street, City, State, ZipCode, and HMOPremium columns. We would like to know the premiums withheld per employee.

Let's start with the formula report. We prepare report labels using employee last and first names, compute values with SUMIFS, apply formatting, insert a skinny row, and add a report total.

For the PivotTable version, we build the following report:

- PT ROWS: LastName, FirstName; VALUES: Sum(HMOPremium)

To better match the formula report, we change the layout to tabular, remove the employee subtotals, repeat the row labels for all items, format the value field, uncheck the row headers style option, update the report headers, and hide the +/- buttons. The resulting PivotTable is a fair reproduction of the formula report.

Going forward, refreshing the PivotTable is quick since new employee names automatically flow from the data table into the report.

CHAPTER CONCLUSION

When replacing formula-based reports with PivotTables, we can use the various layout and design options discussed to closely match the original reports.

Chapter 14: Multiple Value Fields

SET UP

In addition to multiple row fields, PivotTables support multiple value fields. Let's assume that the underlying data source contains several numeric columns, such as amount, shipping, and sales tax. It is easy to include all of them in the report since PivotTables can contain multiple value fields.

HOW TO

Incorporating several value fields is about as easy as you would expect. You simply insert the desired fields into the values area. There are, of course, additional details to explore.

Let's say our exported invoice data contains customer, amount, sales tax, and shipping columns. When we insert customer as a row field and amount as a value field, the layout area looks like Figure 48 below.

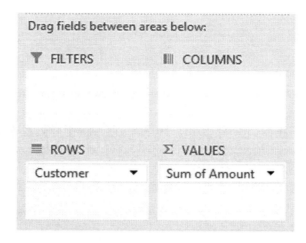

Figure 48

The moment we insert a second value field, such as sales tax, the layout area looks like Figure 49 below.

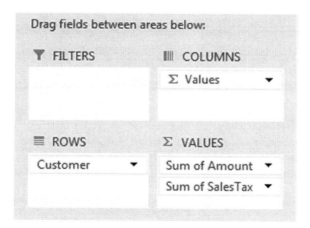

Figure 49

Do you see what just happened there? In addition to the sales tax value field, the PivotTable also includes a new column field named values. This field allows us to control the orientation of the combined value fields. If we leave this field in the columns area, each value field gets its own column. If we move the field to the rows area, we transpose the orientation of the report so that each value field gets its own row.

Another detail concerns grand totals. Although we might expect the PivotTable to automatically sum multiple value fields, it doesn't. If we think about when we've seen grand totals before, we realize that Excel created a grand total row when we inserted a row field, and it created a grand total column when we inserted a column field. These grand totals summarized a single value field, not multiple value fields. Fortunately, it is pretty easy to compute and display the total of several value fields, and we'll explore two approaches in upcoming chapters.

 XREF

Using a PivotTable formula to compute the total of several value fields is discussed in Chapter 15: Calculated Fields. Creating a calculated data column to compute the total of several value fields is discussed in Chapter 24: Data Preparation.

Let's discuss one last detail about multiple value fields. It is obvious that when the underlying data has several numeric columns, we can insert those columns into the values area. What may not be as obvious is that we can drag the same field into the values area multiple times. Even though we can insert it again, why would we want to? The answer is because we can change the math of each value field independently. For example, one value field could display the sum while another could display the average. You'll be able to use this fun technique as you work through the exercises.

EXAMPLES

It is time to build PivotTables with several value fields.

 **PRACTICE**

To work along, please refer to **Multiple Value Fields.xlsx.**

 VIDEO

To watch the solutions video, please visit the Excel University Video Library.

EXERCISE 1—CUSTOMER

In this exercise, we'll create a formula report and a corresponding PivotTable with three value fields.

PRACTICE

To work along, please refer to the Exercise 1 worksheet.

The exported invoice data is stored on the **Data** sheet in the **tbl_data** table and includes InvoiceNum, Date, Customer, Amount, SalesTax, and Shipping columns. Our summary report should display customer, amount, sales tax, and shipping columns.

Starting with the formula-based version, we generate a unique list of customers, sort the list, and then get busy on the formulas. We'll use the SUMIFS function, but before we do, let's enhance our formula-based reporting skills, and implement consistent formulas by locking down table references.

Locking Down Structured Table References

Assuming the first report label is stored in **B12**, we would write the following formula to populate the first value in the amount column:

```
=SUMIFS(tbl_data[Amount],tbl_data[Customer],$B12)
```

We fill the formula down and everything works as expected. When we attempt to populate the tax and shipping columns by filling right, we get incorrect results. A common workaround is to write unique formulas for each column. But as you know, we prefer consistent formulas.

Let's first understand why the formula broke. As we filled right, the table references stopped reflecting the desired ranges. The original formula referenced the amount column for the first SUMIFS argument, and the customer column for the second argument. When we filled right, we intended to reference the sales tax column and the customer column, respectively, but that didn't happen. If we used the fill handle, both table references were treated as relative, which left us improperly referring to the sales tax and amount columns. If we used the fill command or copy/paste, both references were treated as absolute, which left us improperly referring to the amount and customer columns.

XREF

The relative and absolute treatment of structured table references is discussed in Volume 2, Chapter 21.

Now that we know why the formula broke, let's find a solution. When we compare the column order between the report and the data, we notice they are the same: amount, sales tax, and shipping. Since these value columns are in the same order, we can use a relative reference for the amount column, and an absolute reference for the customer column. That way the function arguments will be correct as we fill right, assuming we use the fill handle to do so. If we use the fill handle, Excel treats table column references as relative … unless we use a range operator.

You are familiar with the range operator (colon) because you use it all the time with A1-style range references, such as *A1:B10* and *B:C*. If we use the range operator in a table reference, Excel treats it as absolute. Thus, when using the fill handle to fill right, you will see that table column references are treated as relative, and table range references are treated as absolute. This is true even when the range reference refers to a single column.

The syntax for creating table range references is easy: you just place a colon between the column names and surround them with an additional set of square brackets. For example, in a table named *tbl_data*, you can specify the amount through the sales tax columns as follows:

```
tbl_data[[Amount]:[SalesTax]]
```

You can use the same syntax to reference a single column. For example, the range reference for the customer column follows:

```
tbl_data[[Customer]:[Customer]]
```

This type of range reference is treated as an absolute reference when filled right with the fill handle, the fill command, or copy/paste. This idea is important, so let me highlight it here:

Table range references are treated as absolute when filled right.

Using a table range reference is similar to using the dollar sign $ in a traditional A1-style reference because it locks down the column references. Knowing this, let's revisit our original formula. Our goal was to use a relative reference for the amount column and an absolute reference for the customer column. We can achieve this by updating our original formula as follows:

```
=SUMIFS(tbl_data[Amount],tbl_data[[Customer]:[Customer]],
$B12)
```

Now when we fill right with the fill handle, the amount column reference is relative and updates properly, and the customer range reference is absolute. This technique enables us to use consistent formulas in the report range, and that makes us very happy.

We finish the formula report with number formatting, a skinny row, and report totals.

For the PivotTable version, we build the following:

- PT ROWS: Customer; VALUES: Sum(Amount), Sum(SalesTax), Sum(Shipping)

We finish the report by updating the headers and formatting the value fields. Our PivotTable reflects the same values as our formula report.

Now, let me ask you a question. Could we have computed the formula-based report values with consistent formulas if the column order between the data table and report were different? Let's address this in the next exercise.

EXERCISE 2—ORDER

In this exercise, the column order of our report is different than the data.

 **PRACTICE**

To work along, please refer to the Exercise 2 worksheet.

We'll use the same data as the previous exercise. Our summary report should display customer, shipping, sales tax, and amount, in that order.

Let's start with the formula report. We create the labels by generating and sorting a unique list of customers. We want to use consistent formulas to compute the report values. We've used SUMIFS many times before, but in this case we want it to dynamically adjust the sum range based on the column header. Let's apply functions we've previously explored to accomplish this.

Dynamic SUMIFS

To create a dynamic SUMIFS function, we'll construct the first argument, the sum range, with functions that determine the appropriate data column. We'll enlist the help of our friends INDEX and MATCH, which previously helped us move beyond VLOOKUP.

 XREF

MATCH is discussed in Volume 2, Chapter 6. INDEX is discussed in Volume 2, Chapter 8.

Since the MATCH function returns the relative position of a list item, we can find the report column header in the data table's header row to determine the column to sum. This approach assumes that the headers are consistently named between the data table and the report. The MATCH function provides the proper column to the INDEX function. Previously we learned that the INDEX function returns a cell value from a range at a given position. Additionally, it can return a range reference. Microsoft describes the function as having two forms: the array form and the reference form. The array form returns a cell value, while the reference form returns a range reference. We'll use the reference form to provide the sum range to the SUMIFS function. Let's put these ideas together one step at a time.

It all starts with a basic SUMIFS function. Using structured references, the following formula sums the shipping column:

```
=SUMIFS(tbl_data[Shipping],tbl_data[Customer],$B12)
```

Where:

- **tbl_data[Shipping]** is the sum range
- **tbl_data[Customer]** is the criteria range
- **$B12** is the criteria value

The problem with this formula is that we can't fill it right. Regardless of the fill method or the reference style, we are precluded from filling it right due to the difference in column order. Fortunately, we can rewrite the sum range argument using functions that dynamically determine the proper column.

Let's start with INDEX. To review, the INDEX function has reference, row number, and column number arguments, respectively. Since the shipping column is the sixth data column, the following function could be used instead of the original structured reference:

```
INDEX(tbl_data,0,6)
```

Where:

- **tbl_data** is the entire table reference
- **0** to return all rows
- **6** to return the sixth column

 NOTE

Using zero or blank as the second (third) argument indicates all rows (columns) within the reference.

This function returns the sixth column, which is great for the first report column, but it can't be filled right. Because the column number is expressed as an integer, it won't update as needed. Rather than express this argument as an integer, we'll use the MATCH function to determine the column number.

Assuming the report header is stored in cell **C11**, the following MATCH function will return the column number 6:

```
MATCH(C$11,tbl_data[#Headers],0)
```

Where:

- **C$11** is the report column header
- **tbl_data[#Headers]** is the table's header row
- **0** for exact match

By using the MATCH function to figure out the column number and the INDEX function to return the column reference, we can replace the original structured reference as follows:

```
=SUMIFS(INDEX(tbl_data,0,MATCH(C$11,tbl_data[#Headers],0)),
tbl_data[Customer],$B12)
```

Where:

- **INDEX(tbl_data,0,MATCH(C$11,tbl_data[#Headers],0))** returns the sum range
- **Where:**
  - ○ **tbl_data** is the initial reference
  - ○ **0** returns all rows within the reference
  - ○ **MATCH(C$11,tbl_data[#Headers],0)** returns the column number
  - ○ **Where:**
    - ▪ **C$11** is the report header
    - ▪ **tbl_data[#Headers]** is the table's header row
    - ▪ **0** means exact match
- **tbl_data[Customer]** is the criteria range
- **$B12** is the criteria value

Here is the formula evaluation sequence:

```
=SUMIFS(INDEX(tbl_data,0,MATCH(C$11,tbl_data[#Headers],0)),
```

```
tbl_data[Customer],$B12)
=SUMIFS(INDEX(tbl_data,0,6),tbl_data[Customer],$B12)
=SUMIFS(tbl_data[Shipping],tbl_data[Customer],$B12)
```

Now that the sum range argument is dynamic, the formula works regardless of column order. One last detail we need to address is the second argument, criteria range. Currently it is expressed as a table column reference. Because we love to anticipate the ways in which a user could break our formulas, can you identify the issue here? If the formula is filled with the fill handle, Excel treats the reference as relative. This breaks the formula because the reference is improperly updated as it is filled right. To address this risk up front, we'll specify the column with a table range reference so that Excel treats it as absolute regardless of the fill method, as shown below:

```
=SUMIFS(INDEX(tbl_data,0,MATCH(C$11,tbl_data[#Headers],0)),
tbl_data[[Customer]:[Customer]],$B12)
```

We feel good about this formula because it allows us to adhere to the formula consistency principle.

It takes much less time to create the PivotTable version. We easily build the following report:

- PT ROWS: Customer; VALUES: Sum(Shipping), Sum(SalesTax), Sum(Amount)

We change the report labels to match the formula report, format the values, and we are done.

EXERCISE 3—MONTHS

The purpose of this exercise is to demonstrate how to use multiple value fields with date groups.

 **PRACTICE**

To work along, please refer to the Exercise 3 worksheet.

In this exercise, we'll use a PivotTable to summarize the **tbl_data** transactions by month. We build the following:

- PT ROWS: Month(Date); VALUES: Sum(Amount), Sum(SalesTax), Sum(Shipping)

Wow, this is getting easy! And the best part is that next period, all we'll need to do is paste new data into the table and refresh the PivotTable.

EXERCISE 4—TRANSPOSE

The purpose of this exercise is to demonstrate how to transpose the orientation of the value fields.

 **PRACTICE**

> To work along, please refer to the Exercise 4 worksheet.

In this exercise, we'll use a PivotTable to summarize the *tbl_data* transactions. Our report will ultimately have one column for each customer and a row for each value field. To get started, we'll build the following report:

- PT ROWS: Customer; VALUES: Sum(Amount), Sum(SalesTax), Sum(Shipping)

At this point the report has the correct values but needs to be transposed. To accomplish this, we need to relocate the values field. The values field was auto-generated by Excel the moment we inserted the second field into the values area. Excel placed the values field into the columns area, and thus, each value field got its own column. To transpose the orientation of the value fields, we simply move the values field from the columns area to the rows area. The final step is to move the customer field from the rows area to the columns area. We now have one column for each customer and one row for each value field, which is exactly what we want.

 NOTE

> In practice, we would have saved a step by initially placing the customer field into the columns area. This exercise initially placed it into the rows area as a training illustration.

EXERCISE 5—MULTIPLE

The purpose of this exercise is to demonstrate how to insert the same field into the values area multiple times.

 **PRACTICE**

> To work along, please refer to the Exercise 5 worksheet.

In this exercise, we'll summarize the *tbl_data* transactions and display the amount, count, and average by customer.

Let's begin with the formula report. We generate and sort a unique list of customer labels. We use the SUMIFS function to populate the amount column. For the count column, we use the COUNTIFS function. For the average column, we simply divide the amount by the count. To finish the report, we apply number formatting and add skinny and total rows.

 XREF

COUNTIFS is discussed in Volume 2, Chapter 13.

 NOTE

We could also use the AVERAGEIFS function to compute the average. For more information, please visit the Excel University blog post titled "Conditional Averages with AVERAGEIFS."

For the PivotTable version, we build the following:

- PT ROWS: Customer; VALUES: Sum(Amount), Count(Amount), Average(Amount)

Wow, that was much faster than the formula-based report! We clean it up by formatting the values and updating the report headers.

CHAPTER CONCLUSION

In this chapter we discussed how to insert multiple value fields into our PivotTables. We were even able to insert the same field several times. Understanding how to present multiple value fields helps us build more powerful PivotTables.

Chapter 15: Calculated Fields

SET UP

In this chapter, we'll learn how to display a value field even when the corresponding data column doesn't exist. Wait ... what? Can a PivotTable display a value field when there is no corresponding data column? Yes, when we create a calculated value field. For example, our sales transactions include an amount column but no commission column. Our report needs to display amount and commission values. We'll create a calculated field using a PivotTable formula.

Before we dig into the mechanics, let's consider alternatives. We could compute commission outside of the PivotTable. For example, we could write worksheet formulas that apply the commission rate to amounts retrieved from the PivotTable. In practice, this approach is not recommended for recurring-use workbooks. Since the PivotTable dimensions may change over time, the formulas need to be manually monitored and adjusted accordingly.

Another place to compute commission is in the data source. For example, we could add a new column to the data table that computes commission for each transaction. It is then a simple matter to create a PivotTable with amount and commission value fields. This approach is perhaps my favorite, especially when the data source feeds multiple PivotTables or the math is complex. For example, if the commission rate varies by rep, region, item, or cumulative sales or needs to be retrieved from a worksheet range with a lookup function, this complex math is easily performed with one or more calculated columns in the data table.

 XREF

Creating a calculated data column is discussed in Chapter 24: Data Preparation.

When the math is simple, however, we can work with the data as it comes. This is one of the key worksheet organization concepts explored in Volume 1.

 XREF

Working with data as it comes is discussed in Volume 1, Chapter 16.

Whenever possible, we like to work with data as it comes. Applying the concept here means we preserve the data by not inserting a calculated column in the table. Fortunately, we can compute the commission with a PivotTable formula and leave the data undisturbed.

HOW TO

A calculated field is a value field derived from a PivotTable formula. Think of a calculated field as a column that can operate on other fields. For example, a calculated commission field can apply a commission rate to the amount field. When we create a calculated field, we need to supply the field name and formula to Excel.

 NOTE

Thinking in terms of columns is helpful, but note that PivotTable formulas work in rows as well.

Let's walk through the process by revisiting an exercise from the previous chapter.

ADD

When we were working with multiple value fields, we inserted the amount, sales tax, and shipping fields into the PivotTable. Now we'll sum them with a calculated field. We open the Insert Calculated Field dialog box with the following Ribbon command:

- PivotTable Tools > Analyze > Fields, Items, & Sets > Calculated Field

We enter the desired field name and formula into the dialog box, as shown in Figure 50 below.

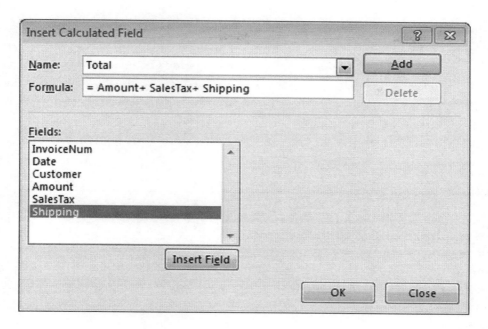

Figure 50

Clicking OK inserts the new calculated field into the values area. That is the basic process, but of course there are a few details to sort through before working on the exercises.

Entering the field's name into the dialog box is straightforward. Stay away from funky characters and avoid names that conflict with other field names or built-in Excel names.

Entering the field's formula into the dialog is also straightforward, although there are a few restrictions. The formula needs to adhere to standard Excel syntax, such as beginning with an equal sign. Similar to other formulas, it can contain operators and constants. Additionally, it can reference PivotTable fields and calculated fields. To reference a field, type the field name, double-click it, or select it and click the Insert Field button. Field names that include spaces need to be enclosed in single quotes. PivotTable formulas support many standard functions, but not all. If you try to use an unsupported function, such as RAND or NOW, you'll get an error message. Worksheet range references aren't allowed, so if you try to include one, you'll get an error message stating that references and names aren't supported in PivotTable formulas. The formula is confined to PivotTable report values and does not operate on individual data source transactions, report subtotals, or grand totals.

EDIT

Once a calculated field is inserted into the report, it is represented by a new field item in the values area. It is essentially another value field and even has its own field settings. To edit a calculated field, open up the Insert Calculated Field dialog and select it from the Name drop-down list. Once selected, you can update the field name or formula.

DELETE

Deleting a calculated field is easy. Since deleting the field and hiding it are closely related, let's cover both options. When we hide a calculated field, we prevent it from appearing in the report but retain its formula. To hide it, just uncheck its checkbox from the field list. When we delete it, we remove it permanently. To delete it, open the Insert Calculated Field dialog and select it from the Name drop-down list. Once selected, click the Delete button.

 NOTE

Please see the Excel help system for additional information on PivotTable formulas.

EXAMPLES

Let's work on the exercises to practice building calculated fields.

 **PRACTICE**

To work along, please refer to *Calculated Fields.xlsx*.

 VIDEO

To watch the solutions video, please visit the Excel University Video Library.

EXERCISE 1—TOTAL

In this exercise, we'll set up a calculated field to sum multiple value fields.

 **PRACTICE**

To work along, please refer to the Exercise 1 worksheet.

The invoice export is stored on the **E1 Data** sheet in the **tbl_e1_data** table and contains InvoiceNum, Data, Customer, Amount, SalesTax, and Shipping columns. We want to summarize amount, sales tax, and shipping by customer.

Starting with the formula report, we generate unique customer labels and use SUMIFS to populate the three report value columns. We create a total column that adds the amount, sales tax, and shipping values. We apply number formatting and add skinny and total rows.

To recreate this report with a PivotTable, we begin with the following:

- PT ROWS: Customer; VALUES: Sum(Amount), Sum(SalesTax), Sum(Shipping)

The PivotTable is similar to the formula report, except it lacks a total column. We'll use a calculated field to create one. In the Insert Calculated Field dialog box, we name the field Total and use the following formula:

```
=Amount+SalesTax+Shipping
```

Bam! Our PivotTable now has a total column and looks like the formula version. We apply a few cosmetic touches by updating the headers and formatting the value fields.

EXERCISE 2—VARIANCE

In this exercise, we'll use a calculated field to compute the difference between budget and actual.

 **PRACTICE**

To work along, please refer to the Exercise 2 worksheet.

The exported account data is stored on the **E2 Data** sheet in the **tbl_e2_data** table and contains AcctNum, Account, Date, Actual, and Budget columns. By account, we would like to view actual, budget, and variance amounts.

To build the formula report, we generate the unique account labels and use SUMIFS to populate the actual and budget columns. Since we are summarizing expenses, we want to report a favorable variance when actual is less than budget and an unfavorable variance when actual is greater than budget. To compute the variance column, we subtract actual from budget values. We confirm that when budget is greater than actual, a positive variance is displayed, and when actual is greater than budget, a negative variance is displayed. We divide variance by budget to create the variance percent column and finish off the report by formatting the numbers and adding skinny and total rows.

To recreate the report with a PivotTable, we start with the following:

- PT ROWS: AcctNum, Account; VALUES: Sum(Actual), Sum(Budget)

To more closely resemble the formula report, the PivotTable needs a few adjustments. We change the report layout from compact to tabular. Better. We remove the account number row field subtotals. Even better. Since the layout looks good, it is time to create the variance columns.

In the Insert Calculated Field dialog box, we name the new field Var and use the following formula:

```
=Budget-Actual
```

Great ... the formula worked! For the variance percent column, we create another calculated field named VarPct and use the following formula:

```
=Var/Budget
```

Hmmm ... it didn't work. Hang on, even though it appears as if the formula didn't work, it really did. We just need to change the value field's number format to percentage. Ah, yes, great ... it worked!

We apply some cosmetic touches by formatting the value fields and updating the headers. We are happy that the report will automatically include any new accounts in the data source when we refresh it next period.

EXERCISE 3—COMMISSION

In this exercise, we'll use a calculated field to compute sales commission for the month.

 **PRACTICE**

To work along, please refer to the Exercise 3 worksheet.

The exported sales transactions are stored on the *E3 Data* sheet in the *tbl_e3_data* table and contain TID, Rep, Date, and Amount columns. We need to summarize sales, and compute commission amounts for each rep.

Starting with the formula version, we generate unique rep labels and use SUMIFS to populate the amount column. For the commission column, we simply multiply sales by our standard commission rate of 3%. We throw on some formatting and add skinny and total rows.

For the PivotTable version, we begin with the following report:

- PT ROWS: Rep; VALUES: Sum(Amount)

To create the sales commission column, we insert a new calculated field. We name it Commission and use the following formula:

```
=Amount*.03
```

Our report now displays commission for each rep. We finish it by formatting the value fields and updating the headers.

CHAPTER CONCLUSION

Calculated fields have many practical applications and enable us to work with the data as it comes.

Chapter 16: Calculated Items

SET UP

A PivotTable formula can create a calculated field or a calculated item. In practice, it is important to know which to use for a given report. As you know, multiple value columns are the result of either multiple value fields or a column field. When we use multiple value fields, the PivotTable displays one column for each value field. Essentially, each report column represents a field. When we use a column field, the PivotTable displays one column for each unique item in that field. Essentially, each report column represents an item.

When determining which PivotTable formula type to use, verify if the report columns represent fields. If so, you'll probably use a calculated field. When the report columns represent items, you'll probably use a calculated item. This idea can be stated slightly differently: to operate on items stored in the same data column, use a calculated item; and to operate on items stored in different data columns, use a calculated field.

 XREF

Column fields are discussed in Chapter 6: Column Fields. Multiple value fields are discussed in Chapter 14: Multiple Value Fields.

HOW TO

In the previous chapter, I asked you to think of a calculated field as a column that can operate on fields. Think of a calculated item as a column that can operate on field items. A calculated item computes results based on the unique report labels that appear in the same data column. Let's clarify this idea with a tangible example and some exercises.

Consider a data source with date, department, type, and amount columns. The type column describes each amount as either budget or actual. In this case, the budget and actual labels are items in the type column, as shown in Figure 51 below.

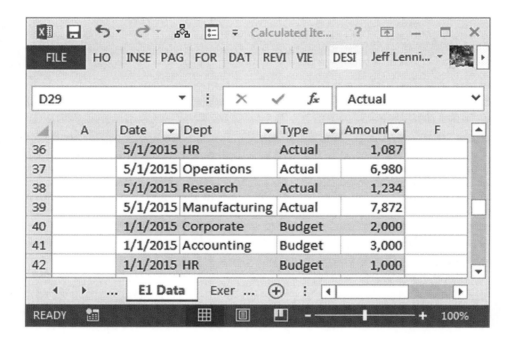

Figure 51

To summarize the data by department and display actual and budget columns, we could set up the following report:

- PT ROWS: Dept; COLUMNS: Type; VALUES: Sum(Amount)

The type column field generates one column for each unique field item, namely budget and actual. We can write a PivotTable formula to compute the variance. Since each report column represents an item, we'll need to use a calculated item.

 NOTE

This is a twist on the exercise we completed in the previous chapter, where actual and budget values were stored in their own data columns and not in a single column. As such, each was placed into the report as a value field, and we used a calculated field to compute the variance.

Creating a calculated item is similar to inserting a calculated field, except that it requires an additional step. Because calculated items operate on items within a field, we must first identify the field. We do this by selecting a cell that contains a report label for the desired field. Since our variance formula needs to operate on the items in the type field, we need to click one of the type column headers: actual or budget.

 NOTE

If you skip this step, unexpected results may occur. For example, you may not be able to select the calculated item command, or the dialog box may not contain the appropriate choices.

After selecting a cell that identifies the desired field, we select the following Ribbon command:

- PivotTable Tools > Analyze > Fields, Items, & Sets > Calculated Item

 NOTE

If the calculated item command is disabled, first click a cell that identifies the desired field.

Confirm the resulting Insert Calculated Item dialog box reflects the intended field in the title, such as Insert Calculated Item in "Type," as shown in Figure 52 below.

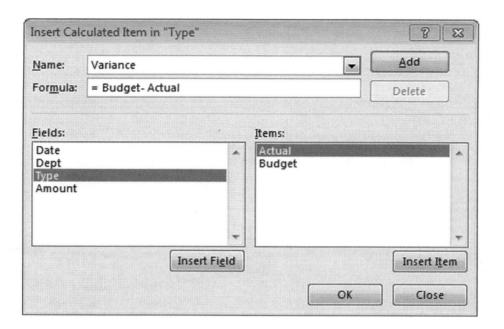

Figure 52

This dialog is similar to the Insert Calculated Field dialog but includes an Items list box, which displays each item in the selected field. For example, the type field contains two items: actual and budget.

 NOTE

> Although you can select other fields and view their items, the formula can only reference items in the field identified in the dialog title.

First, let's name our calculated item Variance. Next, let's write the formula. The syntax is similar to calculated fields, except that instead of operating on fields, the formula operates on field items. For example, to compute variance, we subtract actual from budget, as shown in the following formula:

```
=Budget-Actual
```

The new calculated item is added to the report next to the existing item columns, for example, to the right of the actual and budget columns.

NOTE

You may experience limitations with calculated items, such as being prevented from inserting a new calculated item if the PivotTable contains groups. For additional information, please reference the built-in Excel help system.

Ready to give it a try?

EXAMPLES

Let's work on a couple of exercises to get comfortable building calculated items.

 **PRACTICE**

To work along, please refer to *Calculated Items.xlsx.*

 VIDEO

To watch the solutions video, please visit the Excel University Video Library.

EXERCISE 1—VARIANCE

In this exercise, we'll compute the difference between budget and actual values by department.

 **PRACTICE**

To work along, please refer to the Exercise 1 worksheet.

The exported transactions are stored on the *E1 Data* sheet in the *tbl_e1_data* table and contain Date, Dept, Type, and Amount columns. The type column describes each row as representing actual or budget data. We would like to summarize the data by department and display actual, budget, and variance columns.

Starting with the formula version, we generate and sort a unique list of department labels and use SUMIFS to populate the actual and budget columns. The formula for the variance column is easy: we simply subtract actual from budget. We finish up by formatting the cells and adding skinny and total rows.

For the PivotTable version, we begin with the following:

- PT ROWS: Dept; COLUMNS: Type; VALUES: Sum(Amount)

Our first cleanup task is to remove the Grand Total column, which has been created automatically and adds the budget and actual columns. Do you remember how to remove it? Uncheck the Show grand totals for rows checkbox in the in the PivotTable Options dialog box or use the related Ribbon command.

Our next task is to create the variance column with a PivotTable formula. Since the report columns represent items, we'll create a new calculated item. We identify the type field by clicking the budget or actual column header cell and open the Insert Calculated Item dialog box.

 NOTE

Before opening the Insert Calculated Item dialog box, please be sure to select a column header cell, such as the budget or actual label cell, and not a value cell, such as one that contains an amount.

We name the calculated item Variance and use the following formula:

```
=Budget-Actual
```

Our report now has a variance column! We finish the report by applying a few cosmetic touches, such as formatting the values and updating the headers.

EXERCISE 2—FIELDS

In this exercise, we'll compute the difference between budget and actual values by account.

 **PRACTICE**

To work along, please refer to the Exercise 2 worksheet.

The exported transactions are stored on the *E2 Data* sheet in the *tbl_e2_data* table and contain AcctNum, Account, Date, Actual, and Budget columns. We would like to summarize the data by account and display actual, budget, and variance columns.

Starting with the formula report, we generate and sort a unique list of account number and name labels and then use SUMIFS to compute the actual and budget columns. We use simple math to compute the variance column. We format the values and insert skinny and totals rows.

To reproduce this report with a PivotTable, we begin with the following:

- PT ROWS: AcctNum, Account; VALUES: Sum(Actual), Sum(Budget)

We change the report layout from compact to tabular, remove subtotals for the account number field, and turn off the +/- buttons. We'll use a PivotTable formula to create the variance column. Should we use a calculated field or a calculated item? Yes, a calculated field! Why? Because the report columns represent fields. That is, the budget and actual values are stored in separate data columns rather than in a single data column. We insert a new calculated field that subtracts actual from budget, format the values, and update the report labels.

CHAPTER CONCLUSION

PivotTable formulas help us work with the data as it comes. Knowing when to use calculated fields or calculated items is key. When report columns represent fields, we probably want a calculated field. When they represent items, we probably want a calculated item.

Chapter 17: Show Values As

SET UP

So far, we have summarized value fields with simple math functions, such as sum or count. In addition to these basic aggregate functions, Excel provides many options for displaying value fields. For example, we can show the values as a percentage of the report total or as a running total. This chapter explores some of the many options.

HOW TO

When we were grouping and subtotaling value fields, we used the Summarize Values By tab within the Value Field Settings dialog box. It is time to explore the Show Values As tab, as illustrated in Figure 53 below.

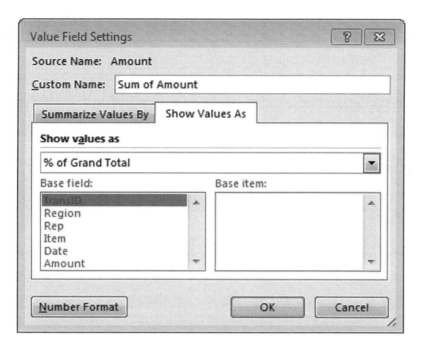

Figure 53

 XREF

Grouping and subtotaling is discussed in Chapter 9: Groups and Subtotals.

The Show Values As tab has a drop-down field that includes many fun options, including % of Grand Total, as displayed in the screenshot above.

In addition to using the Value Field Settings dialog box, you can right-click a value cell and select the desired option from the Show Values As shortcut menu item.

Rather than provide comprehensive detail for all options, I'll just highlight my favorites:

- % of Grand Total—displays report values as a percentage of the report total. There are similar options for % of Row and % of Column totals as well.

- % of Parent Total—displays each report value as a percentage of its group subtotal. There are similar options for % of Parent Row and % of Parent Column as well.

- Running Total In—displays a running subtotal.

The exercises use my favorite options, but please explore the others, as they may be helpful in your reports.

 NOTE

Beginning with Excel 2013, you can use this feature to count distinct rows if the source range is added to the data model. Please see the Excel help system for additional details or check out the Excel University blog post titled "Count Distinct Values in an Excel 2013 PivotTable."

EXAMPLES

Let's work on a few exercises.

 **PRACTICE**

To work along, please refer to **Show Values As.xlsx**.

right click

 VIDEO

To watch the solutions video, please visit the Excel University Video Library.

EXERCISE 1—PERCENT OF TOTAL

In this exercise, we'll show report values as a percentage of the total.

 **PRACTICE**

To work along, please refer to the Exercise 1 worksheet.

The exported transactions are stored on the **Data** sheet in the **tbl_data** table and include TransID, Region, Rep, Item, Date, and Amount columns. Our report should summarize the transactions by item and display amount and percent of total columns.

Starting with the formula report, we generate and sort a unique list of item labels and use SUMIFS to populate the amount column. For the percent of total column, we use a simple formula that divides each value by the total. We slap on some formatting, add skinny and total rows, and are good to go.

For the PivotTable version, we begin with the following:

- PT ROWS: Item; VALUES: Sum(Amount)

Creating the percent of total column is a two-step process. We need to insert the amount field into the values area again and then show its values as a percentage of the grand total. Do you remember how to insert a field multiple times? Yes, by dragging it.

 XREF

Inserting the same field multiple times is discussed in Chapter 14: Multiple Value Fields.

After the amount field is inserted into the values area again, our report has two amount columns. For one of them, we show the values as a percentage of the grand total by using the Value Field Settings dialog box or the right-click shortcut, as discussed above. We apply formatting and update the report headers.

EXERCISE 2—PERCENT OF PARENT

In this exercise, we'll show values as a percentage of the parent field. Our report will display sales by region and within each region by rep. We will display the sales of each rep as a percentage of the region, that is, of the parent field.

 **PRACTICE**

To work along, please refer to the Exercise 2 worksheet.

Our report will summarize the transactions from the previous exercise by region and rep and will also display amount, percentage of total, and percentage of region columns. We begin with the following report:

- PT ROWS: Region, Rep; VALUES: Sum(Amount)

We just need to add the percentage of total and percentage of region columns. We insert the amount field into the values area again and then show its values as a percentage of the grand total. Now we want to view each rep's performance relative to their region, so we insert the amount field again. Since the row field order is region and then rep, the region field is the rep field's parent. If we switch the order of the row fields, then the relationship switches accordingly. To see the performance of each rep as a percentage of their region, we need to show values as a percentage of the parent total. There are three options related to showing values as a percentage of parent:

- Percent of Parent Row Total

- Percent of Parent Column Total

- Percent of Parent Total

Use the Percent of Parent Row Total option to operate on row fields. Try this option now, and you'll notice that each rep value is reflected as a percentage of the region, which is great. But you'll also notice that the region subtotals are displayed as a percentage of their parent, which is the report total. This presentation is fine, but we would prefer to see 100% in each region subtotal row. So let's move on.

Use the Percent of Parent Column Total option to operate on column fields. This option would have been appropriate if we had inserted a field into the columns area. Since we didn't, let's examine the final option.

The Percent of Parent Total option operates on either row or column fields and allows us to define a base field. What's a base field? Here, the base field allows us to define the parent. The previous two options used the field order to determine the parent.

 NOTE

Since this option calculates a percentage of the parent total, the base field represents the parent field used in the denominator. Other options use the base field in ways relevant to their calculations.

Go ahead and try this option now. Use region as the base field and notice that rep values and region subtotals are presented as a percentage of the base field. Since all report values use the selected base field as the denominator, each region subtotal row displays 100%, which is our preferred presentation. The report needs a few cosmetic touches. We use the following Ribbon command to move the subtotals to the bottom of each region:

- PivotTable Tools > Design > Subtotals > Show all Subtotals at Bottom of Group

We format the value fields and update the report headers. Nice.

EXERCISE 3—RUNNING TOTAL

In this exercise, we'll experiment with the running total option.

 **PRACTICE**

To work along, please refer to the Exercise 3 worksheet.

Using data from the previous exercise, we'd like to create a report that displays monthly sales and year-to-date amounts. We begin with the following:

- PT ROWS: Month(Date); VALUES: Sum(Amount)

 XREF

Grouping date fields by month is discussed in Chapter 9: Groups and Subtotals.

To create the year-to-date column, we insert the amount field into the values area again and show its values as a running total. The running total is computed for the selected base field, which in our case is the date field, because we'd like to show the running total by month. Beautiful! We format the value fields and update the headers to Period, Month, and YTD, and we are done!

CHAPTER CONCLUSION

In addition to simple aggregate functions such as sum and count, Excel provides other ways to display value fields. We've only worked with a few of the many options, so please explore the others, as they may be useful in your reports.

Chapter 18: Sorting

SET UP

This chapter examines the details of sorting so you can display reports in the desired order. Many users assume that PivotTables are automatically sorted by the first row field, and that there is nothing further to explore. Surprisingly, there are many subtle details to consider when creating efficient recurring-use workbooks.

default is manual

HOW TO

The default sort order for PivotTables is manual, which allows you to manually place items in the desired order. Initially, the report is displayed in ascending order based on the first row field. This initial order isn't maintained over the life of the PivotTable. For example, if the report is later refreshed, any new row labels are placed at the bottom of the report rather than in alphabetical order. For single-use reports, this default is probably just fine, but we want to be intentional about the sort order of our recurring-use reports.

The key is to sort the PivotTable, not the worksheet. If you sort the worksheet, you'll need to sort it each period. If you sort the PivotTable, the sort order is automatically applied each period. It seems that sorting gets easier in each new version of Excel. Here are a few ways to sort a PivotTable:

- Interact with row and column label drop-down controls

- Right-click a cell in the desired field and select the sort order from the shortcut menu

- Activate the PivotTable and use one of the following Ribbon commands:

o Home > Sort & Filter

o Data > AZ

o Data > ZA

o Data > Sort

 NOTE

The sort descriptions change depending on the data type. For example, the ascending description for a date field is Sort Oldest to Newest, while a numeric field is Sort Smallest to Largest.

Let's dig into the row and column label drop-down controls for a moment. In the report header, Excel automatically places a drop-down control on the row and column label cells. For example, Excel placed drop-down controls in cells *B17* and *C16* in the PivotTable shown in Figure 3. The drop-down controls provide a convenient way to sort and filter the report.

 XREF

PivotTable filtering is discussed in Chapter 19: Filtering.

When the report layout is tabular or outline, each row field gets its own column and drop-down, which makes it easy to sort by the desired field. In compact view, there is a single column and drop-down for all row fields. Expanding the drop-down enables you to select a row field and define the sort. Selecting the More Sort Options item reveals the Sort dialog box shown in Figure 54 below.

Figure 54

The Sort dialog provides a few options, including the ability to sort by a value field. Although using the right-click shortcut menu is probably a faster way to sort, it is good to be aware of this dialog box. The More Options button reveals the More Sort Options dialog box, which provides additional settings, such as automatically sorting when the report is refreshed and identifying a specific sort column.

Before we move on, let's review the manual sort option shown in Figure 54. As discussed, this is the default option. It enables you to click and drag items to arrange them. You can reposition an item by selecting its cell, hovering the cursor over the bottom cell border, and dragging the item to the desired location. In addition, you can move an item by typing its label into the new location. To clarify, if the value you type matches an existing item label, Excel repositions the item. Otherwise, Excel uses the value as the new item label. We'll do an exercise to practice manual sorting. Speaking of exercises, are you ready?

 NOTE

Beyond the options presented, additional sorts are available, including left-to-right and custom lists. Please consult the Excel help system for additional information.

EXAMPLES

Let's practice sorting with a few hands-on exercises.

To work along, please refer to **Sorting.xlsx**.

To watch the solutions video, please visit the Excel University Video Library.

EXERCISE 1—ASCENDING

In this exercise, we'll sort by account number.

To work along, please refer to the Exercise 1 worksheet.

The exported accounting transactions are stored on the *E1 Data* sheet in the *tbl_e1_data* table and contain TransID, AcctNum, Account, Date, and Amount columns. Since we'd like the summary to display the accounts in financial statement order, rather than in account name order, we'll sort by account number.

For the formula version, we generate and sort the account number and name labels and use SUMIFS to populate the amount column. We finish up by formatting the report values and adding skinny and total rows.

For the PivotTable version, we begin with the following:

- PT ROWS: AcctNum, Account; VALUES: Sum(Amount)

We are off to a good start but need to address a few issues. First, let's change the layout from compact to tabular. Ah, yes, that's much better. Next, let's remove the account number subtotals. Great. Since a PivotTable is initially displayed in ascending order by the first row field, our report currently has the desired order. But there are a few details to unpack.

If the account name field had been first, the report would have been displayed by account name. But to our surprise, if we tried sorting by account number (the second row field), Excel would not return the desired sort order. If we sorted by account number, Excel would sort by account number within each account name group, and since there is only one account number for each account name, we wouldn't notice a change.

This idea may make more sense if we consider a different example. If the first row field was region and the second was rep, then sorting ascending or descending by the rep field would tell Excel to sort the list of reps within each region group in ascending or descending order, accordingly. The PivotTable sort order is controlled by the field order, where the first sort is by the first row field, and so on. This built-in behavior is an example of the structure limits we discussed when comparing formula and PivotTable reports. Although we are restricted to sorting the overall PivotTable report by the first row field, we can easily sort a formula-based report by any column.

 NOTE

A quick Internet search will provide creative workarounds to this PivotTable sort restriction, including setting up a custom list or duplicating the field in the data source, inserting it into the rows areas twice, and then hiding its worksheet column.

Let's finish the PivotTable by applying a few cosmetic touches. Since we don't want people trying to expand/collapse the account numbers, we remove the +/- buttons. Last, we format the values and update the report headers. We are done ... right? Let's find out.

Let's pretend we need to update the report next period. We'll manually add the following new transaction to the data table:

- TransID = 2550

- AcctNum = 5045

- Account = Print Ads

- Date = 12/28/2016

- Amount = 500

We navigate back to the PivotTable and refresh it. Although the new transaction flows into the PivotTable, it does not appear in the expected order. Since the transaction's account number is 5045, we expect it to appear in account number order, namely, between accounts 5041 and 5050. But it doesn't. Instead it appears at the bottom of the report. Now, I've gone to great lengths to create this dramatic moment, so here is the big finish that ties it all together. Even though the report is initially displayed in ascending order, the default sort is manual, not ascending. With a manual sort, new items appear at the bottom of the report. To ensure new items appear in ascending order, we need to change the sort from manual to ascending. Going forward, we know that new accounts will appear in order.

EXERCISE 2—DESCENDING

In this exercise, we'll apply a report filter and sort by the value field.

 **PRACTICE**

To work along, please refer to the Exercise 2 worksheet.

The exported accounting data is stored on the *E2 Data* sheet in the *tbl_e2_data* table and contains TransID, AcctNum, Account, DeptNum, Dept, Date, and Amount columns. To facilitate our analysis, we want to create an interactive report that summarizes the SG&A expenses. We should be able to pick an account and view the subtotals by department. The report should be sorted descending by amount so that the departments with the highest expenses for the selected account appear near the top.

Starting with the formula report, we generate a unique list of department labels. For the report filter, we use data validation to create a drop-down list of accounts.

 XREF

Using data validation to create report filters is discussed in Volume 2, Chapter 24.

The SUMIFS function computes the report values based on the selected account. We format the cells, and add skinny and total rows. The report is looking good, and now it's time to test the filter.

Let's select the travel account and make a couple of observations. As expected, departments with no travel expenses continue to appear in the report and reflect a zero value. Since the report retains the original department order, we need to manually sort descending by amount using the relevant Ribbon command or shortcut. After the sort, we confirm that the department labels have been repositioned to reflect the desired report order.

Let me ask you a question. Did it make you a little nervous to manually sort the report? It made me nervous because I was afraid I would accidentally break something. I wasn't sure if the headers or total row would be included in the sort, and I wasn't sure if the formulas and report labels would stay lined up. Fortunately, nothing broke when we sorted, so we are good … right? Well, let's pick a different account, such as telephone. Even though the report values update accordingly, the sort order doesn't. That means we need to manually sort the report, which causes us to get nervous again. Additionally, sorting the report is a manual step, and as you know, we prefer to eliminate manual steps. Let's see how a PivotTable behaves.

We begin with the following report:

- PT ROWS: Dept; VALUES: Sum(Amount); FILTERS: Account

Let's use the report filter to select the telephone account and make a couple of observations. As expected, the report only includes departments with expenses. Since the report is displayed ascending by department name, we sort the report descending by amount. Now, let's pick another account, say, travel. Bam! The report values and the sort order are automatically updated. I'm not sure about you, but I'm loving PivotTables!

EXERCISE 3—MANUAL

In this exercise, we'll perform a manual sort.

 **PRACTICE**

To work along, please refer to the Exercise 3 worksheet.

The data is stored in the *tbl_e3_data* table on the *E3 Data* sheet and contains TransID, Date, Item, Region, and Amount columns. We would like to summarize the data by item and place each region in its own column.

Starting with the formula-based report, we generate and sort a unique list of item labels. For the column headers, we enter the region codes N, S, E, and W. The region order is consistent throughout all reports at our company, and this report should be no exception. We populate the report values with SUMIFS, format the cells, and add a skinny and total row.

For the PivotTable version, we begin with the following:

- PT ROWS: Item; COLUMNS: Region; VALUES: Sum(Amount)

This report is similar to the formula version with one exception, the column order. Our PivotTable displays the region columns in alphabetical order as E, N, S, and W, which, unfortunately, doesn't conform to our company standards.

Since the default sort is manual, we are free to rearrange the column orders as needed. One way is to drag the columns into the desired position. Go ahead and try it now. Another way is to type the region code directly into the desired cell. This method feels a little funny at first, because you type the region code into a cell that contains a different region code. Please try it now and watch Excel swap the region columns as desired. Remember, if you enter a region code that doesn't exist, for example North, Excel changes the label instead. Go ahead and try this now. After you are done playing around, finish the report by arranging the region columns in the proper order.

CHAPTER CONCLUSION

It is important to understand that the default PivotTable sort is manual. Knowing how to sort the report as needed enables us to control the presentation and helps us improve the efficiency of our recurring reports.

Chapter 19: Filtering

SET UP

This chapter continues and expands upon our previous discussion about filtering. So far we have created report filters, but there are more ideas and techniques to cover.

 XREF

Report filters are discussed in Chapter 7: Filter Fields.

Filtering allows us to control which data source rows are included in the report. Beyond allowing us to interactively analyze the data, filtering has strategic implications. This capability enables us to export all transactions that tie to an expected amount, such as the annual total, and display a subset, such as a single quarter. Filtering data makes it easy to check our work because the data source total ties out to the expected amount, even though our report may only include some of the transactions.

We can apply the same idea to historical data. Rather than replacing prior-period transactions stored in the data table, we can paste-append new transactions to the table and then simply filter the report to reflect the desired period. This makes it easy to reference prior-period amounts as needed.

In practice it is often more convenient to retrieve subsets from a single data source than to combine multiple data sources. For example, we can easily build several PivotTables from a single data source and filter each to present the desired subset of information. Let's build our proficiency right now by jumping into the mechanics.

HOW TO

We'll discuss the following methods of filtering PivotTables:

- Report filters

- Field filters

- Slicers

Even though we previously covered report filters, there is one fun detail we have yet to explore.

REPORT FILTERS

Since we've already discussed the mechanics of setting up report filters, we will proceed directly to the fun part.

 XREF

> Setting up report filters is discussed in Chapter 7: Filter Fields.

Once a PivotTable report filter is created, a previously disabled Ribbon command is enabled. It is Show Report Filter Pages, accessed from the following Ribbon icon:

- PivotTable Tools > Analyze > Options > Show Report Filter Pages

 NOTE

> The Options icon is split. Clicking the left side, labeled Options, reveals the Options dialog box. Clicking the right side, which has a little drop-down arrow, reveals a shortcut menu with the Show Report Filter Pages command. This command is disabled until the PivotTable contains a filter field.

The resulting Show Report Filter Pages dialog box allows you to select the desired report filter field. Click OK, and bam: Excel creates a new report sheet for each item in the selected field. Let's consider the following scenario: you create a PivotTable report, and it looks good. Because you used the region field as a report filter, you can easily review each region. Satisfied with the values, you want to create a new report sheet for each region. Rather than creating each report manually, you use the show report filter pages command. Excel instantly inserts a new worksheet for each region that contains a copy of the original PivotTable filtered for the region. This command offers a fast way to generate a new report sheet for each region.

NOTE

There are a variety of ways to deliver reports, for example, printed to paper, as a PDF, or as an Excel file. If delivered as an Excel file, by default the user will be able to change the filter selection. Possible options to prevent this include worksheet protection and unchecking the Save source data with file option.

 XREF

Worksheet protection is discussed in a subsequent volume.

FIELD FILTERS

We can also filter the report with the same row and column field drop-downs we used previously to sort the report. When using these drop-downs to filter recurring reports, be aware of the option to automatically include new items in the manual filter, which is available in the Field Settings dialog box for the field (as shown in Figure 27). If this box is left unchecked, new items will not appear in the report. If checked, any new items automatically flow into the report. Depending on your needs, this option may be useful.

 NOTE

There are additional options to explore in the field filter drop-down, including label and value filters that provide choices such as Begins With, Contains, and Greater Than. When the PivotTable contains multiple row or column fields, selecting a label cell before expanding the drop-down populates the Select field option with the desired field.

SLICERS

The most spectacular filtering method is slicers. First introduced with Excel 2010, slicers provide a graphical filter interface and are especially valuable when delivering digital reports.

 NOTE

In Excel 2010, slicers filter PivotTables. Beginning with Excel 2013, they can also filter tables.

You insert a slicer by activating the PivotTable and clicking the following Ribbon icon:

- PivotTable Tools > Analyze > Insert Slicer

Select the desired field or fields in the resulting Insert Slicers dialog box, and Excel sets up a slicer for each selected field, such as the department field slicer shown in Figure 55 below.

Figure 55

Filtering with a slicer is easy. Just select the item, and Excel instantly applies the filter. You include multiple items by holding down the Ctrl key while selecting. Clear the filter with the remove all filters icon in the upper-right corner of the control.

Slicers offer several benefits. Slicers make it easy to filter the report and see which items are currently selected. Because slicers are independent of the report layout, we can insert filtered fields into any area to create the desired report. For example, we can insert the department field used to create the slicer above into the rows, columns, filters, or values layout areas. If we use department as a row field and select multiple departments, the report displays each department separately. If we use department as a report filter field, the combined values are displayed instead. This flexibility enables us to easily filter and display the desired report values.

We also have the option to connect several reports to a single slicer. When we interact with the slicer, all connected reports are filtered accordingly. Remember our Start Here sheet from previous volumes? The Start Here sheet is designed to store settings, and this slicer would be a perfect addition to it.

To connect multiple reports to a slicer, select the slicer and use the following Ribbon command:

- Slicer Tools > Options > Report Connections

The Report Connections dialog box displays the PivotTables in the workbook that share a cache with the PivotTable used to create the slicer. Simply select the desired PivotTable reports and click OK. Now the slicer updates all connected PivotTables.

Slicers have numerous design and style options, such as color, number of columns, button sort order, caption, and button dimensions. Spend some time exploring the various settings available on the following Ribbon tab:

- Slicer Tools > Options

You can resize and move the slicer by activating it and clicking and dragging the borders. You can delete it by right-clicking it and selecting Remove or by selecting the slicer and pressing the Delete key. You can cut it from one worksheet and paste it into another with standard cut/paste commands.

 NOTE

The timeline control was introduced in Excel 2013. It is similar to a slicer and designed to work with date fields.

Let's go ahead and jump into some exercises.

EXAMPLES

Please work through the following exercises to practice.

 **PRACTICE**

To work along, please refer to *Filtering.xlsx.*

 VIDEO

To watch the solutions video, please visit the Excel University Video Library.

EXERCISE 1—DEPARTMENT

The purpose of this exercise is to compare report and field filters. We've previously used a report filter to control which transactions flow into a report. For example, we inserted the department field into the filters area and were able to select and display any department. If we had selected multiple departments, they would have been included in the report, but as a combined total. Now we'll use a field filter so that each selected department is displayed individually.

 **PRACTICE**

To work along, please refer to the Exercise 1 worksheet.

The exported data is stored in the *tbl_data* table on the *Data* sheet and contains TransID, AcctNum, Account, DeptNum, Department, Date, and Amount columns. We want to create an interactive report that contains a department filter and displays the account values.

Let's begin with the formula-based report. We generate and sort the account labels. We create a department filter with data validation and use our dear friend SUMIFS to populate the values. To test it out, we select a department and confirm that the report values have updated as expected. But what if we want to include two departments? We can't do this because data validation only allows one selection. Since PivotTable filters allow multiple selections, let's build the PivotTable version.

We'll start with the following report:

• PT ROWS: Account; VALUES: Sum(Amount); FILTERS: Department

We can easily filter for any department by using the report filter. In addition, by expanding the report filter and checking the multiple items checkbox, we can select two or more departments. When we select multiple departments, the report values reflect the sum of the selected departments. To display each department's values rather than the combined sum, we need to use a field filter rather than a report filter. Let's move the department field from the filters area to the rows area, as follows:

• PT ROWS: Department, Account; VALUES: Sum(Amount)

In the updated report, we can see that all selected departments are listed. We can pick and choose which departments are displayed by using the field filter. So when you need your report to show the combined totals of selected items, use a report filter. When you need your report to display values for each selected item, use a field filter.

EXERCISE 2—MONTH

The purpose of this exercise is to use column field filters.

 **PRACTICE**

To work along, please refer to the Exercise 2 worksheet.

We want to summarize the data from the previous exercise by account and display one column for each month in the first quarter. Let's begin with the following report:

- PT ROWS: Account; COLUMNS: Month(Date); VALUES: Sum(Amount)

We now use the column field drop-down to filter the report to include January, February, and March. Easy enough.

EXERCISE 3—SLICER

In this exercise, we get to play with slicers!

 **PRACTICE**

To work along, please refer to the Exercise 3 worksheet.

We want to summarize the data from the previous exercise by account and make it super easy to filter the departments. We begin by building the following report:

- PT ROWS: Account; VALUES: Sum(Amount)

Our report currently includes transactions for all departments. To easily filter by department, we insert a slicer for the department field. To test the slicer, we pick a department and notice the report values update as expected. Now let's explore a bit further.

Notice that we used the department field as a slicer, but did not include the department field in the report. Slicers are independent and filter the report even if we've not inserted the field into the report. If we insert the department field into the rows area above the account field, any selected departments get their own section in the report. If we move the department field to the columns area, each selected department gets its own column. If we move the department field to the filters area, the sum of the selected departments is displayed. Since the field location is independent of the slicer, we can structure the report as needed.

EXERCISE 4—MULTIPLE CONNECTIONS

In this exercise, we'll connect multiple reports to a single slicer.

 **PRACTICE**

To work along, please refer to the Exercise 4 worksheet.

The slicer we created in the previous exercise filters the PivotTable that we created in the previous exercise. Let's build the following new report from the same data source and then update the previous exercise's slicer so that it filters both reports:

- PT ROWS: Account; COLUMNS: Month(Date); VALUES: Sum(Amount)

To update the slicer so that it filters both reports, we need to add our new PivotTable to the slicer connections. We select the slicer created in the previous exercise and then click the following Ribbon icon:

- Slicer Tools > Options > Report Connections

From the Report Connections dialog box, we simply check the new report's checkbox. To test it out, we select a few departments in the slicer and notice that both reports are filtered accordingly and that the report totals agree ... wow!

EXERCISE 5—FILTER PAGES

have have ge a Filter Field selected

In this exercise, we'll show report filter pages.

 **PRACTICE**

To work along, please refer to the Exercise 5 worksheet.

We want to summarize the data from the previous exercise by account and display one column for each month. Since we want to generate a report for each department, we set up a report filter using the department field. We get to work and quickly build the following report:

- PT ROWS: Account; COLUMNS: Month(Date); VALUES: Sum(Amount); FILTERS: Department

When we are satisfied with the report, we are ready to generate a copy for each department. Although we aren't sure if we'll ultimately print the reports to PDF or paper or whether we'll deliver them as

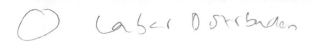

digital Excel files, our goal is to create one report for each department. Rather than filter the report one department at a time, we'll delegate the task to Excel.

We click the little drop-down on the right side of the Options Ribbon icon and select the Show Report Filter Pages item. In the resulting Show Report Filter Pages dialog box, we select the department field and click OK. Excel gets busy and inserts a new worksheet for each department. Each new sheet contains a copy of the original PivotTable that is filtered for the department. Wow, this is a fast way to generate report copies.

 NOTE

If the department field is removed from the filters layout area, the Show Report Filter Pages command will be disabled because it is only available when the PivotTable includes a report filter.

CHAPTER CONCLUSION

It is important to consider filtering when developing an overall workbook strategy and workflow. The data source can contain all transactions that sum to an expected amount and feed one or more filtered reports. Slicers provide an easy way to create an interactive digital report.

Chapter 20: Hybrid Reports with GETPIVOTDATA

SET UP

At this point we feel comfortable using the PivotTable feature to build many of our reports. But what if we encounter a specific report that we can't build with a PivotTable? Perhaps we can't get the layout or format just right. Although we'd love to use a PivotTable to aggregate the data, we need the flexibility of a formula-based report because it has no structure restrictions. We need the best of both worlds ... we need a hybrid report.

The idea is to create a formula-based report that retrieves values from a PivotTable. In a sense the PivotTable becomes an intermediate step, and the data flows from the data sheet to the PivotTable to the formula report. Since we prefer retrieving values with lookup functions rather than direct cell references, we have become familiar with lookup functions such as VLOOKUP, INDEX, and MATCH. It is time to explore another. The GETPIVOTDATA function is a lookup function designed specifically to retrieve PivotTable values. GETPIVOTDATA will return a value from a PivotTable even if the value's cell location changes when the report is refreshed.

HOW TO

The GETPIVOTDATA function retrieves a desired value from a PivotTable. It uses row and column items to identify the value to return. When I use this function, I think about it like this:

Select this value field, from this PivotTable, where this field is equal to this value, and where...

The function arguments are set up in this order. We identify the value field and then the PivotTable. The remaining arguments come in pairs: first the criteria field and then the criteria value. The function syntax follows:

```
=GETPIVOTDATA(data_field,pivot_table,[field1],[item1],…)
```

Where:

- **data_field** is the name of the value field, expressed as a text string

- **pivot_table** is the upper-left cell of the PivotTable, expressed as a cell reference

- **[field1]** is the name of the criteria field, expressed as a text string

- **[item1]** is the name of the criteria item, expressed as a text string

- **…**up to 126 pairs of field and item names are supported

🔲 NOTE

If the arguments don't reference a value that is displayed in the PivotTable, the function will return an error.

Although we could write the function by hand, we don't need to. Fortunately, we can easily insert a GETPIVOTDATA function by typing an equal sign into a blank cell and selecting a PivotTable value.

🔲 NOTE

The default automatically generates GETPIVOTDATA functions. This behavior can be turned on or off with the following Ribbon icon: PivotTable Tools > Analyze > Options > Generate GetPivotData.

For example, consider the PivotTable shown in Figure 56 below, which summarizes sales data by rep.

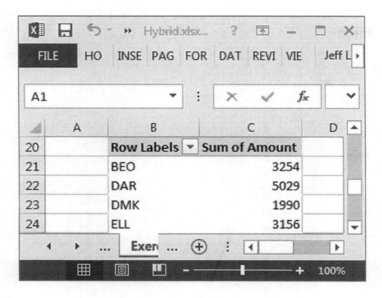

Figure 56

Let's say we want to retrieve the amount for rep BEO from the PivotTable. After entering an equal sign into a blank cell, we simply select cell *C21*. Excel automatically inserts the appropriate function, shown below:

```
=GETPIVOTDATA("Amount",$B$20,"Rep","BEO")
```

Where:

- **"Amount"** is the name of the value field, expressed as a text string

- **B20** is the upper-left cell of the PivotTable, expressed as an absolute cell reference

- **"Rep"** is the name of the criteria field, expressed as a text string

- **"BEO"** is the name of the criteria item, expressed as a text string

Retrieving a single value is pretty easy. But what if we want to fill the formula down and retrieve values for other reps? For example, consider the formula-based report shown in Figure 57 below.

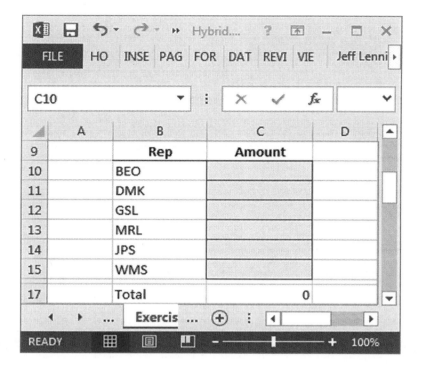

Figure 57

To create the formula for the first rep in cell *C10*, we enter an equal sign and then select the corresponding PivotTable value. Excel populates the cell with the following formula:

```
=GETPIVOTDATA("Amount",$B$20,"Rep","BEO")
```

When we fill the formula down, we notice that the same value is returned for all cells. Since the item argument is the text string BEO, the value for BEO is returned for all cells. Fortunately, we can simply replace the text string with a cell reference. We manually edit the existing formula as follows:

```
=GETPIVOTDATA("Amount",$B$20,"Rep",B10)
```

As we fill this updated formula down, we are glad to see the expected rep values appear in our report.

 NOTE

Formula-based reports, even those built with GETPIVOTDATA, require that we manually add new items.

Before we head into the exercises, let's talk about when and how we could use the GETPIVOTDATA function. I use the following report preference hierarchy. When I need to build a report, my first preference is a PivotTable because new items automatically appear in the report, reducing errors and improving efficiency. If I can't build the report with a PivotTable due to structure restrictions, my next preference is a formula-based report. For example, since a PivotTable isn't a good fit for complex financial statements, I'll break out the SUMIFS function and a mapping table. When I can't accomplish my objectives with either of these methods, I'll explore the technique of creating a hybrid report that uses the GETPIVOTDATA function to retrieve values from an intermediate PivotTable.

Here are a few examples of when you can use the GETPIVOTDATA function:

- When you analyze the underlying transactions with a PivotTable, and may already have established calculated fields and items, the GETPIVOTDATA function ensures that the formula report reflects the PivotTable values and alleviates the need to reproduce the logic with the SUMIFS function or other complex formula.

- When you prepare a dashboard or key performance indicator report, this function conveniently enables you to retrieve selected values from one or more PivotTables and present them in a small space. The PivotTables enable you to review the values and drill down into the details as needed. You can ensure the total of the PivotTable ties to the expected amount, even though only selected values flow to the dashboard.

- When you want to display values from two or more PivotTables in a single report, this function makes it easy. For example, you could create a variance report that pulls actual and budget values from two different PivotTables built on two different data sources.

It is time to work through the exercises.

EXAMPLES

Please open Excel and practice retrieving values from a PivotTable with the GETPIVOTDATA function.

 **PRACTICE**

To work along, please refer to **Hybrid.xlsx**.

 VIDEO

To watch the solutions video, please visit the Excel University Video Library.

EXERCISE 1—SINGLE VALUE

This is our first warm-up exercise.

 **PRACTICE**

To work along, please refer to the Exercise 1 worksheet.

The exported data is in the *tbl_data* table on the *Data* sheet and contains TransID, Region, Rep, Item, Date, and Amount columns. We would like to create a PivotTable to summarize the data by rep and use the GETPIVOTDATA function to retrieve the amount for a specific rep.

We begin with the following report:

- PT ROWS: Rep; VALUES: Sum(Amount)

Our PivotTable includes all transactions and reps, and the total agrees with the table. To retrieve the amount for DMK, we type an equal sign into a blank cell and select the applicable PivotTable cell. Excel automatically writes the GETPIVOTDATA function for us (thank you Excel), and the formula successfully retrieves the desired amount.

 NOTE

Excel automatically writes the GETPIVOTDATA function if the PivotTable Tools > Analyze > Options > Generate GetPivotData option is checked.

Next period, when we paste new data into the table and refresh the PivotTable, the GETPIVOTDATA function automatically retrieves the updated DMK value.

EXERCISE 2—MULTIPLE VALUES

In this exercise, we'll express the GETPIVOTDATA item argument as a cell reference so we can fill the formula down.

 **PRACTICE**

To work along, please refer to the Exercise 2 worksheet.

Using the data from the previous exercise, we'll build a PivotTable and retrieve values for several reps. We begin with the following report:

- PT ROWS: Rep; VALUES: Sum(Amount)

We note the upper-left cell of the PivotTable is *B20* and confirm that the total agrees with the table. After setting up labels for the selected reps, we have Excel write the GETPIVOTDATA function for the first rep, BEO, and the resulting formula follows:

```
=GETPIVOTDATA("Amount",$B$20,"Rep","BEO")
```

Where:

- **"Amount"** is the value field

- **B20** is the upper-left corner of the PivotTable

- **"Rep"** is the lookup field, the rep field

- **"BEO"** is the lookup item, the selected rep

If we were to fill this formula down to complete the report, the amount for BEO would be returned for all cells because the item argument is a static text string. The fix is simple. We edit the formula and change the item argument to a relative cell reference pointing to the rep label in *B9*, as follows:

```
=GETPIVOTDATA("Amount",$B$20,"Rep",B9)
```

We fill this updated formula down and are pleased to see that it works as expected.

EXERCISE 3—MULTIPLE SOURCES

Let's create a report that incorporates values from multiple PivotTables. The overall idea is to create a formula-based report that compares actual sales to the forecast. Since the actual and forecast amounts are summarized in separate PivotTables, we'll use the GETPIVOTDATA function to retrieve them as needed.

 **PRACTICE**

To work along, please refer to the Exercise 3 worksheet.

Since we summarized the actual sales transactions in the previous exercise, we'll use the PivotTable on the *Exercise 2* worksheet for our actual data in this exercise. The forecast data is stored in the *tbl_fc* table on the *E3 Data* sheet. On the *E3 PT* worksheet, we summarize the forecast data by rep by building the following report:

- PT ROWS: Rep; VALUES: Sum(Amount)

We begin the formula report by generating the rep labels. To populate the report values, we retrieve actual amounts from the PivotTable on the *Exercise 2* sheet and forecast amounts from the PivotTable on the *E3 PT* sheet. We use the technique of replacing the default GETPIVOTDATA item argument with a cell reference so the formulas can be filled throughout the report. To finish the report, we compute the variance and highlight positive and negative variances with green and red conditional formatting.

CHAPTER CONCLUSION

Before Microsoft introduced the SUMIFS function in Excel 2007, multiple condition summing was more difficult, and I used the hybrid technique more frequently. Although this technique seems less important now than in earlier versions of Excel, I wanted to cover the GETPIVOTDATA lookup function so you know how to use it to retrieve values from PivotTables if needed.

This chapter concludes the Working with PivotTables section. My goals were to provide a working knowledge of PivotTables and demonstrate the features that enable you to replicate formula-based reports. These chapters weren't designed to deliver an exhaustive review of everything the PivotTable feature has to offer. The PivotTable feature contains plenty of other details you can investigate. I'll leave you with a quick inspirational story.

In a live Excel session, I asked participants to share their experiences with PivotTables. One participant quickly raised his hand and said, "Jeff, I took one of your Excel classes a couple years ago, and you taught me about PivotTables. After I converted many of my reports to PivotTables, my job got really easy and boring." He delegated his manual reporting tasks to Excel and then had a lot of free time … wow! I love that story because it dramatically illustrates the efficiency gains that are possible with Excel.

OBTAIN > PREPARE > SUMMARIZE

Gain efficiency by optimizing data flow and examining how data is obtained, prepared, and summarized.

Chapter 21: Web Data

SET UP

So far we have focused on summarizing data with PivotTables. In this section we expand our discussion and consider how data enters the workbook and flows to the summary. We'll explore features, functions, and techniques that help us obtain, prepare, and summarize data.

Let's begin by considering the way we obtain data from external sources. In this chapter we'll retrieve data from perhaps the largest external data source of all, the World Wide Web.

Before we dig into the mechanics, let me ask you a question. What would you bring if you were going to be stranded on a deserted island? For me, I think I would bring Excel. I mean, it's the only program you need. It even has a built-in web browser! Wait, what? Yep. Excel has its own web browser. This web browser is similar to other web browsers, such as Internet Explorer, Chrome, and Safari, because it allows you to surf the web. Additionally, it enables you to select a data range on a web page and import it into an Excel worksheet. This feature provides a convenient way to obtain data from the web.

HOW TO

One way to obtain data from a web page is to copy and paste it into a worksheet. If you don't need to repeat this task in the future, the copy/paste method may work just fine. However, a more interesting approach is to leverage Excel's external data feature. When used in recurring-use workbooks, this feature makes it easy to refresh the worksheet with updated web data.

For example, let's say we use foreign currency exchange rates in a workbook that we regularly update. Because exchange rates change all the time, we want an easy way to retrieve the current rates. Rather than doing a copy/paste each time we need to update, we can use Excel's external data feature. To retrieve external web data, we open Excel's web browser with the following Ribbon command:

- Data > From Web

This command launches the browser in a dialog box named New Web Query. The next step is to navigate to the web page with the exchange rates by typing in the web address or clicking hyperlinks. Since we've decided to grab the data from Google, we simply type *google.com / finance* in the address field.

One notable difference between Excel's web browser and other web browsers is that it identifies importable data tables with a yellow arrow icon. As we scroll down Google's finance page, we see many yellow icons identifying the tables we can import. After we click the yellow icon for the currencies table, Excel changes it to a green check icon and shades the selected table, as shown in Figure 58 below.

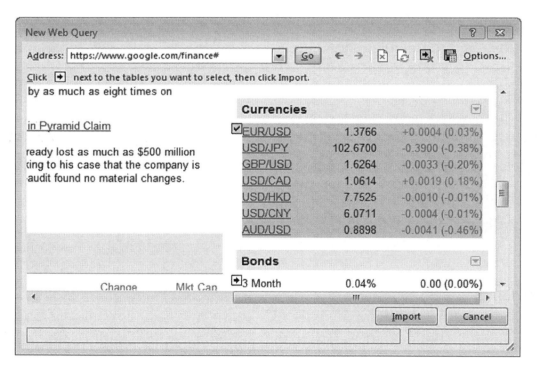

Figure 58

Clicking the Import button reveals the Import Data dialog box. After we identify the location of where we want to send the imported data, Excel inserts the exchange rates into our worksheet, as shown in Figure 59 below.

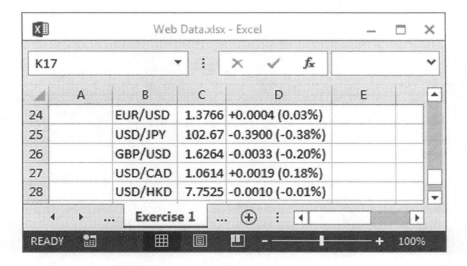

Figure 59

The best part is that we can easily retrieve current rates going forward without launching Excel's browser. When we refresh the range, Excel retrieves the web page's current values. To refresh the range, we right-click a value cell within the imported range and select Refresh from the shortcut menu or select a value cell and the following Ribbon icon:

- Data > Refresh All > Refresh

 NOTE

While I prefer to initiate a web import from within Excel as described above, you can also initiate it from within Internet Explorer. Browse to the desired web page, right-click the web table, and select Export to Microsoft Excel. Be aware that although this approach does establish a refreshable connection, it sends data to a new, rather than existing, workbook.

Now that we've successfully retrieved web data, we are ready to use it with functions and features. We first need to determine how Excel stores the external data in our worksheet, for example in a named range or a table. When we retrieve web data, Excel stores it in a named range. As we'll see in the next chapter, when we retrieve data from an Access database, Excel stores it in a table.

Because Excel stores the data in a named range, our instinct is to convert the range into a table so we can benefit from three table properties: auto-expansion, structured references, and auto-fill. Aw, snap … when we try to convert the range into a table, we get an error message. But don't panic. We can still enjoy the benefits of these three table properties. We just need to understand a few details, and we'll begin by examining named reference scope.

Named Reference Scope

We covered named references long ago, and because we've used them in numerous practice exercises, we won't rehash the basic mechanics now.

Named references are discussed in Volume 1, Chapter 7.

It is time to examine named reference scope. Each name, whether we created it manually or Excel created it with the external data feature, has a scope. The scope tells Excel where you intend to use the name, such as on a specific worksheet or throughout the workbook. When you manually create a name, the default scope is workbook, and thus the name appears in the Name box, the Paste Name dialog box, and in the auto-complete list on all worksheets in the workbook. You could instead tell Excel you intend to use the name only within a specific worksheet by changing the default scope to the desired sheet. In this case the name would appear in the Name box, the Paste Name dialog box, and the auto-complete list only within the specified sheet. You define the scope in the New Name dialog box when you initially create the name, as shown in Figure 60 below

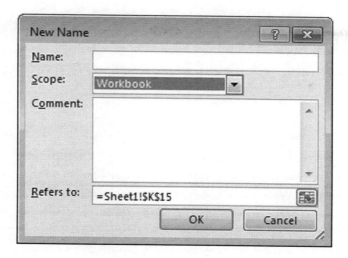

Figure 60

Excel prevents you from changing the scope once the name is defined. When you create a name by typing it into the Name box, the default workbook scope is applied. To specify the scope, create the name with the name manager. You can view the scope of existing names by inspecting the name manager.

 NOTE

Excel allows you to use duplicate names in a workbook, provided they each have a different scope.

Excel stores external web data in a named range that has a worksheet, not workbook, scope. When you try to reference the range from another sheet, the name won't appear in the auto-complete list, the Name box, or the Paste Name dialog box. If you try to type the name directly into your formula, you'll get an error. And, since you can't change the scope of a name, you are stuck ... or are you? Of course not.

As you know, we can refer to a cell or range on another sheet by preceding the reference with the sheet name and an exclamation mark. For example, referring to cell *B2* on *Sheet1* would be accomplished with the reference *Sheet1!B2*.

 XREF

Preceding references with sheet name and exclamation point is discussed in Volume 1, Chapter 3.

Since our external web data was automatically stored on the *Sheet1* worksheet in a range named *finance*, we can reference it in functions and features throughout the workbook with *Sheet1!finance*. We can type the reference manually or let Excel insert it automatically by selecting the range. Now that we know how to use an external data range with a worksheet scope, it's time to learn how our external range can enjoy benefits typically associated with tables, namely auto-expansion, structured references, and auto-fill.

Auto-Expansion

The beauty of auto-expansion is that new transactions are automatically included in formulas and features. When we store data in a table, the table auto-expands when we add new transactions. The external data range feature exhibits similar behavior. When we refresh the range, new transactions flow into the worksheet, and the name expands accordingly. Any formulas that reference the name automatically incorporate new transactions.

Structured References

Another benefit associated with tables is structured references. Structured references enable us to refer to areas within the table, such as a specific column. Unfortunately however, named references that have been set up manually or automatically by the external data feature don't provide structured references. But the good news is that we can simulate structured references using a familiar function.

Let's say we retrieve web data that is stored in a range named *finance* in the *Sheet1* worksheet. The data range has three columns. If we want to sum the values in all columns, we could use the named reference in a SUM function. But let's say we want to sum the values in a specific column, such as the second column. Because structured references don't apply to named ranges, we'll need to use a worksheet function to return the desired column reference. Can you think of a function that returns a range reference? Yes, the INDEX function. We can use the INDEX function to return a subset of the entire range. For example, to sum the second column, we could use the following formula:

```
=SUM(INDEX(Sheet1!finance,0,2))
```

Where:

- **INDEX(Sheet1!finance,0,2)** returns all rows of the second column

- **Where:**

    o **Sheet1!finance** is the external web data range

    o **0** means all rows

    o **2** means the second column

The INDEX function allows us to simulate structured references by returning an area within the named range, such as a specific column or row.

 NOTE

The MATCH function works well with the INDEX function, and we can use them together to dynamically select the column based on the header, as illustrated in Chapter 14: Multiple Value Fields.

Auto-Fill Formulas

Another benefit we enjoy when using tables is that formulas are automatically filled down for new rows. Fortunately, this behavior is also available for external data ranges stored in named references.

Although this behavior is not enabled by default, you can easily enable it. After you import data, open the External Data Range Properties dialog box by right-clicking a value cell within the range and selecting Data Range Properties from the shortcut menu or by selecting a value cell and clicking the following Ribbon command:

- Data > Properties

Check the Fill down formulas in columns adjacent to data checkbox. Any formulas Excel finds on the first data row in columns that are adjacent to and right of the range are filled down when refreshed.

 NOTE

Formulas are filled down, but values are not. If you need to fill a value down, write a formula that returns the value, such as =5.

Before we get to the exercises, let's work through some frequently asked questions.

FREQUENTLY ASKED QUESTIONS

Here are several common questions about using Excel to obtain web data.

Can I automatically refresh this data?

Yes. In addition to manually refreshing the data as discussed above, you can tell Excel to automatically refresh the range when the workbook is opened or at set intervals while it is open. Both of these options are available in the External Data Range Properties dialog box referenced above.

How do I edit the range?

To edit the range, right-click a value cell and then select Edit Query from the shortcut menu. This will open the Edit Web Query dialog box and allow you to uncheck the original table and select a different one.

 NOTE

> If possible, avoid changing the default range name. However, if you do need to change it, use the External Data Range Properties dialog box rather than the name manager, prior to using it in formulas or features.

How do I delete the range?

Select the entire range and press the Delete key. Excel will clear the cell contents and prompt you to confirm that you'd like to permanently remove the connection and disable future refreshes. You also can delete the connection by selecting a value cell and then the following Ribbon icon:

- Data > Connections

From within the resulting Workbook Connections dialog box, select the desired connection and click Remove.

Can I prevent Excel from changing the column widths?

Yes. Excel automatically adjusts the column widths to accommodate imported data. If you like your column widths the way they are, turn off this behavior within the External Data Range Properties dialog box.

How do new transactions flow into the worksheet?

The number of transactions retrieved may vary each time you refresh an external data range. Fortunately, Excel allows you to control how to handle the changing number of rows. Within the External Data Range Properties dialog box, you'll see the following three options:

- *Insert cells for new data, delete unused cells*—When new transactions create more rows than before, Excel inserts additional worksheet cells to accommodate the new data. When there are fewer rows, Excel deletes the unused cells.

- *Insert entire rows for new data, clear unused cells*—When new transactions create more rows than before, Excel inserts entire rows to accommodate the new data. When there are fewer rows, Excel clears the unused cells.

- *Overwrite existing cells with new data, clear unused cells*—When new transactions create more rows than before, Excel replaces the values in existing cells. When there are fewer rows, Excel clears the unused cells.

For the most part, I prefer to insert entire rows for new data and place external data ranges on their own sheets.

Can I retrieve values from online documents, such as PDF or Excel files?

No. Excel's web browser retrieves data that is displayed within web pages, but not within files, such as PDF, CSV, or Excel attachments. To gain access to information stored within online files, download the files to your computer and open as normal.

Can I retrieve data from a secure web page?

Although the external data feature can usually retrieve data from a secure web page, the individual website's security settings may prevent a future refresh. Because security varies from site to site, with some allowing you to stay logged on and others automatically logging you off after a period of time, the only way to know for sure is to give it a try. Some web-based accounting systems do support Excel web queries, so it may be worth contacting their support team to find out.

Can I retrieve data from my intranet?

Yes. Excel's external data feature retrieves data appearing in your browser and works with both public websites and intranets.

What if the web page changes?

If the values on a web page change, Excel will retrieve the new values. If the structure or URL of the page changes, then the external range may no longer refresh, and you will need to edit the connection or create a new one.

Can I use the external range with data validation?

Yes. To create an in-cell drop-down using data validation, we need to provide a reference that returns a single-column sheet range. If the external data range includes multiple columns, we need a way to reference just one of them. Here's a question for you: if we have a named range, created manually or with the external data feature, which function can return a single-column reference? Yes, INDEX.

We'll use the INDEX function to return a single-column reference and provide it to the data validation feature. Since data validation won't let us enter the formula directly, we'll revisit a technique we used back in Volume 1 when we wanted to use a table column with data validation. We set up a name that referenced the desired column and then used that name with data validation.

We'll do the same here and create a name that refers to a formula that returns the desired column reference. This type of name is often called a named formula. As we've discussed previously, names can refer to cell references, range references, constants, and formulas. For example, to use the first column of the *finance* range on **Sheet1**, we would set up a new name, such as **dd_er**, that refers to the formula:

```
=INDEX(Sheet1!finance,0,1)
```

Where:

- **Sheet1!finance** is the entire range

- **0** means all rows within the range

- **1** means the first column within the range

To create the drop-down, we use data validation and allow a list equal to the named formula **dd_er**. This technique works for named ranges created manually or automatically by the external data range feature.

What about stock quotes?

There are many web pages that provide stock quotes, so start with your favorites and see if they are compatible with Excel's external data feature. Google and Yahoo's finance pages usually work well, and both provide current and historical quotes. Additionally, Microsoft provides several built-in web queries that include the details Excel needs to retrieve specific data from the Internet. For example, the built-in MSN MoneyCentral Investor Stock Quotes query enables us to store ticker symbols in a worksheet and retrieve current stock prices. We'll use this web query in an exercise so you can experiment with it.

What else should I know?

My goal was to provide a basic introduction to retrieving web data. This chapter does not provide an exhaustive resource on the topic, and many additional capabilities are worth investigating. Feel free to explore this feature and use the built-in Excel help system for additional information.

EXAMPLES

Let's practice retrieving web data.

 **PRACTICE**

To work along, please refer to **Web Data.xlsx.**

 VIDEO

To watch the solutions video, please visit the Excel University Video Library.

EXERCISE 1—EXCHANGE RATES

In this exercise, we'll retrieve currency exchange rates from a web page.

 **PRACTICE**

To work along, please refer to the Exercise 1 worksheet.

Let's use Google's finance page to retrieve the exchange rates. We open Excel's web browser and enter the address *google.com/finance* into the address field. We scroll down the page until we see the currencies table on the right. We click the yellow icon and confirm that the currency table is shaded. We click the Import button, tell Excel where the data should be placed, and bam, the data is returned to our worksheet. Whenever we want to retrieve current rates, we simply refresh the range ... wow!

 NOTE

Excel's browser sometimes displays error alerts for web pages. If so, the data may still import as expected, and dismissing the error alert is fine. If the data doesn't import properly, try using an alternate web page to obtain the data, or perhaps try the same web page later, and it may work.

EXERCISE 2—PRICE LIST

In this exercise, we'll use the retrieved data in formulas.

 **PRACTICE**

To work along, please refer to the Exercise 2 worksheet.

We'll use the exchange rates from the previous exercise to convert our dollar-denominated price list to euros. We can retrieve the proper rate from the external range with a traditional lookup function such as VLOOKUP. We'll store the corresponding label, EUR/USD, in a cell, and reference the label in our formula. The external data feature automatically named the range *finance,* and assigned a local worksheet scope. Since we want to pull the rate into a different sheet, we'll precede the name with the worksheet name *Exercise 1*. For example, if we store the label in cell *B13*, we can retrieve the exchange rate from the web data range with the following formula written in cell *C13*:

```
=VLOOKUP(B13,'Exercise 1'!finance,2,0)
```

Where:

- **B13** is the lookup value, the EUR/USD currency label

- **'Exercise 1'!finance** is the lookup range

- **2** indicates the exchange rate column

- **0** means exact match

We apply this exchange rate to the price list to create the Euro column and finish the report by formatting each column with the appropriate currency symbol.

EXERCISE 3—STOCK QUOTES

In this exercise, we'll use the Existing Connections icon to access the built-in MSN MoneyCentral Investor Stock Quotes connection and retrieve quotes for ticker symbols stored in the worksheet.

 **PRACTICE**

To work along, please refer to the Exercise 3 worksheet.

We begin by entering the ticker symbols, separated by commas, into a worksheet cell. For example, let's enter MSFT, GOOGL, AAPL into the cell. Next, we click the following Ribbon icon:

- Data > Existing Connections

From the Connections tab in the resulting Existing Connections dialog box, we select MSN MoneyCentral Investor Stock Quotes and click the Open button.

NOTE

Depending on how Excel was installed, the built-in MSN MoneyCentral IQY files may not be installed, and thus the MSN MoneyCentral Investor Stock Quotes option may not appear in the Existing Connections dialog box. If this happens, search for IQY on the Excel University blog and download the missing IQY files.

In the resulting Import Data dialog box, we tell Excel where to place the data and click OK. Excel asks for the ticker symbols by displaying the Enter Parameter Value dialog box. Although we could manually enter the ticker symbols into this dialog, we'll simply reference the cell that contains them. Since we want Excel to use this ticker cell each time we refresh, we check the Use this value/reference for future refreshes checkbox. Since we want Excel to automatically refresh the range when we update the cell value, we check the Refresh automatically when cell value changes checkbox. We click the OK button, and bam, our worksheet now contains the current stock prices for each of our stock symbols.

Excel includes other built-in web queries in the Existing Connections dialog box, so feel free to explore them and use the Excel help system for more information.

 NOTE

Each web query has a corresponding IQY text file that provides Excel with the web service details. The IQY files are typically stored in the My Documents\My Data Sources directory.

CHAPTER CONCLUSION

Excel's built-in web browser enables us to retrieve data from a vast external data source. This feature's utility increases as more of the data we work with is available online and delivered through a web browser.

Chapter 22: External Data

to a table in Excel or to a pivot table directly

Automation

SET UP

We began our external data journey by retrieving web data in the previous chapter. Now that you have taken one step, will you take another with me? Excel is capable of retrieving data from a variety of different data sources, including web pages, databases, text files, SQL servers, and other ODBC (Open Data Base Connectivity) compliant sources. Although we don't have time to cover them all, the basic principles and techniques that apply to one apply to others.

In this chapter, you'll retrieve data from the popular desktop database application Microsoft Access. The skills you'll develop will help prepare you for retrieving data from other data sources as well.

We have already built many formula-based and PivotTable reports that have summarized worksheet data. The underlying assumption has been that the exported data was copied and pasted into the worksheet. Perhaps we opened our accounting system and ran a report, query, or transaction listing. We exported the data and pasted it into our reporting workbook. In practice, this is often our only option. When it is, we do our best to optimize efficiency, for example by storing the data in a table.

As we discovered in the previous chapter, we can get data into a workbook with the external data feature, which basically replaces the manual export/copy/paste process. Since our goal is to eliminate manual tasks from recurring processes, we'll try to use the external data feature to retrieve data when possible. After we set up the connection, pulling data into the workbook in subsequent periods is as simple as clicking the Refresh button. Formulas and reports that reference the data range update accordingly.

My goal is to provide enough basic information to get you started. If this feature turns out to be relevant to your work, please continue to explore its many wonderful capabilities.

HOW TO

Think of corporate accounting systems as having two parts. The frontend is the application that provides the user interface, screens, and reports. The backend is the database that stores the transactions. Sometimes both parts are developed by the same company, but developers often build their applications on a third-party database engine. The external data feature retrieves transactions from the backend database.

 NOTE

> Although Excel ships with drivers for connecting to many common databases, you may need to check with manufacturers of other databases for their corresponding drivers.

In general, Excel can retrieve transactions from data sources located on your computer's network. For example, if you try to retrieve data from your company's database, there is a good chance Excel can connect, since it is probably located on your local area network (LAN). However, Excel most likely won't be able to retrieve data stored in a database on another LAN, such as a client's database, since your computer probably isn't connected to the remote network.

NOTE

> Corporate IT security settings may prevent connections to the production database. If so, your IT department may provide other options, such as a reporting or replication version of the database or access through third-party tools.

Let's walk through the mechanics with a tangible example. We want to build a report based on data from our accounting system. Rather than export/copy/paste as we've done in the past, we'll obtain the data with the external data feature. Our accounting system stores transactions in an Access database. We select a cell in the worksheet that indicates the desired location of the imported data. The Data Ribbon tab contains numerous icons in the Get External Data section, as follows:

- *From Access*—simplified Access database retrieval

- *From Web*—retrieve with Excel's web browser

- *From Text*—retrieve from delimited or fixed width text files, such as CSV or TXT files

- *From Other Sources*—retrieve from a wide variety of data sources

- *Existing Connections*—view and edit existing external data connections

Since our data is stored in an Access database, one way to retrieve it is to click the From Access button, select the table, and click OK. However, this option provides only a subset of the external data feature's capabilities and can create file restrictions. To use the full power of the external data feature, we'll retrieve our data with Microsoft Query instead. Microsoft Query? Yep. It's a utility that sits between the external data source and Excel. It basically obtains and processes the transactions, passing the resulting data set to the worksheet. Let's click the following Ribbon icon:

- Data > From Other Sources > From Microsoft Query

This brings up the Choose Data Source dialog box, as shown in Figure 61 below.

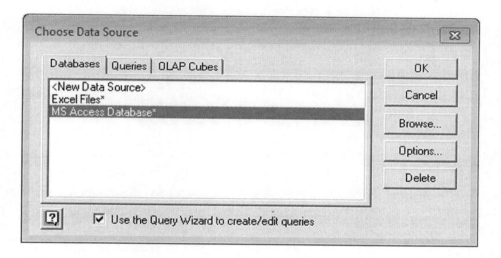

Figure 61

Since we are trying to connect to an Access database, we double-click MS Access Database or select it and click OK.

 NOTE

Clicking the Browse button is different than selecting MS Access Database and clicking the OK button. This dialog provides many connection options, and they are worth exploring if this feature is relevant to your work.

The resulting Select Database dialog prompts us for the location of the database, as shown in Figure 62 below.

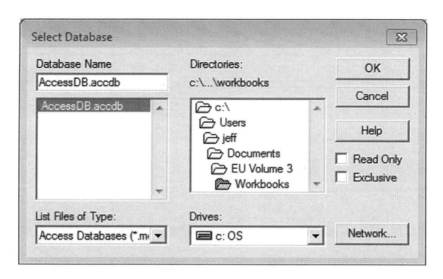

Figure 62

We use the dialog box to browse to the location of the database. Please note that this dialog box was developed a while ago, and lacks the features of modern dialogs. For example, to navigate to a different drive, you'll need to use the Drives field. Since the Directories list box doesn't include Windows libraries and shortcuts, to navigate to My Documents you'll need to head to C:\Users and then locate the My Documents folder within your user folder.

Once we've identified the database, we click OK and are presented with the Query Wizard dialog box. The first step in the wizard allows us to identify the columns we would like returned to the worksheet. The left side of the dialog lists the tables and queries, and the right side lists the selected columns. Simply select or expand the desired table or query and use the arrow buttons to identify the desired columns. For our report, we select all columns from the *tbl_invoices* table, as shown in Figure 63 below.

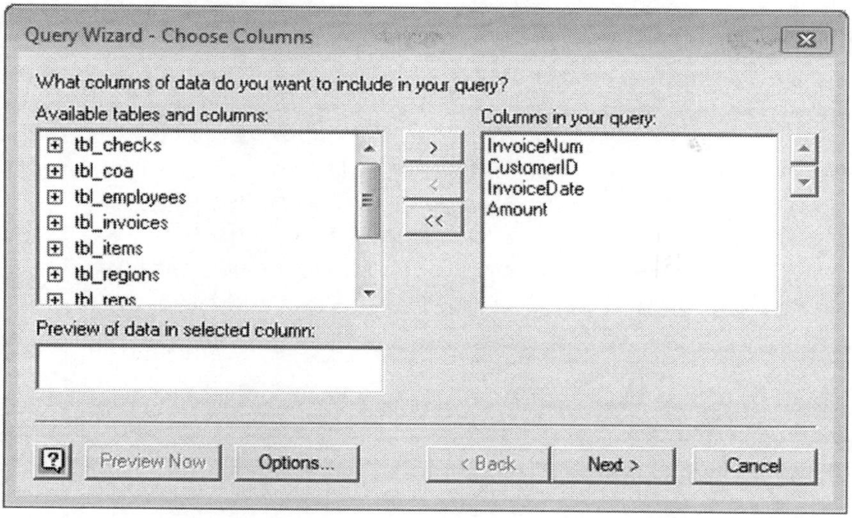

Figure 63

In the next step of the wizard we use filters to identify the rows we want to retrieve, as shown in Figure 64 below.

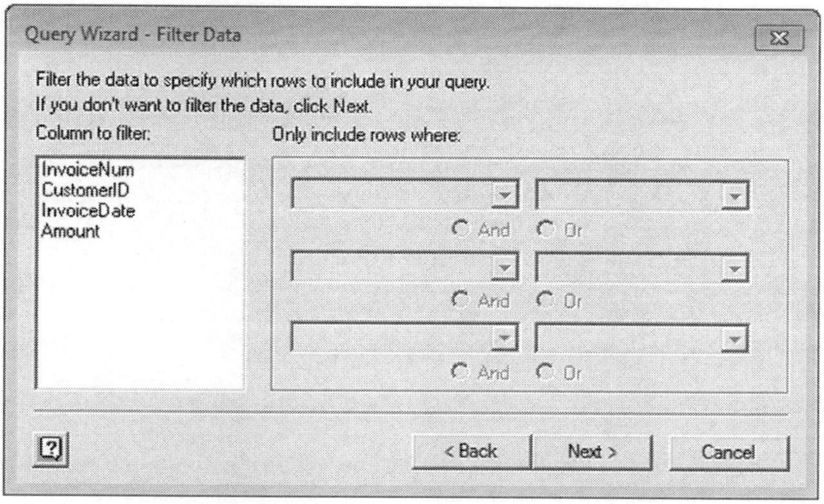

Figure 64

We can limit the rows that are returned to the workbook by selecting a column to filter, choosing a comparison operator, and then choosing or typing a value. For our report, we'll use all rows, so we simply advance to the next step of the wizard.

The next step of the wizard allows us to specify the sort order. For our report, we aren't concerned about the sort order, so we simply advance to the next step.

In the final step of the wizard, shown in Figure 65 below, we can either immediately return the data to Excel or view the data/edit the query in Microsoft Query.

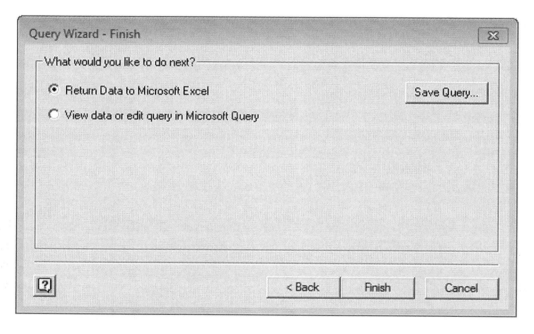

Figure 65

 NOTE

If you use the Save Query button to save the options specified in the wizard, it is easy to use them in other workbooks by selecting Browse in the first step of the wizard (Figure 61).

We can open Microsoft Query now or later to edit the query, for example by adding calculated fields, aggregating rows, or providing additional filters or parameters. For our report, we return the data to

Excel. We are presented with the Import Data dialog box, shown in Figure 66 below, where we can indicate how and where the data should be returned.

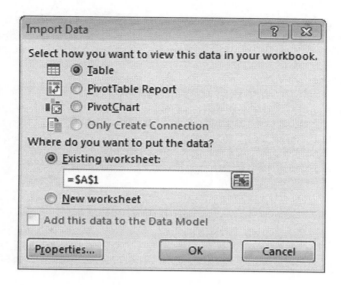

Figure 66

We can return the data to a table in an existing or new worksheet and then summarize the table data with a formula-based or PivotTable report. In addition to sending the external data to a table, we can send it to a PivotTable. Rather than pulling data into a table and building the report from the table, we send the data directly to the PivotTable report. We can also send the data directly to a PivotChart, which is an interactive chart that aggregates transactions. For our report, we return the data to a table.

 XREF

PivotCharts are discussed in Chapter 26: Getting Graphic.

Since the data flows into the worksheet and is stored in a table, we easily summarize the data and complete our report. In future periods, we can easily refresh the external data table by right-clicking any value cell in the table and selecting Refresh from the shortcut menu or by selecting a value cell and then the following Ribbon command:

- Data > Refresh All > Refresh

Excel goes to the external data source and retrieves transactions based on the column, row, and sort order selections. Since the table will expand to include new rows, our report will automatically include any new transactions. With this technique, we can update our reports by refreshing the external data range. This feature helps improve the efficiency of our recurring-use reports.

FREQUENTLY ASKED QUESTIONS

Here are several common questions about the external data feature.

Is this connection one-way?

Yes, the external data range feature is a one-way, read-only connection. Any changes to the values in Excel do not get pushed into the database.

When I refresh, are new transactions appended, or is the entire range replaced?

Excel retrieves transactions based on the selections made during the wizard and replaces the existing data table with them. As a result, transactions added to the external data source since the last refresh are appended to the table, transactions deleted from the source are removed, and edited transactions are updated. You can't assume that the same transactions will land in identical table cells each refresh, so avoid referring to them with direct cell references. Because the data is replaced, any manual edits made to the table data are lost.

How can I modify the query?

You modify the query by stepping through the wizard and making changes to the previous selections. In the final step of the wizard, you can launch Microsoft Query if needed.

Probably the quickest way to edit the query is to right-click any value cell in the table and select Table > Edit Query from the shortcut menu. You can also click the Edit Query button on the Definition tab of the Connection Properties dialog box. There are numerous ways to open this dialog box, including:

- Selecting a value cell and then the Data > Refresh All > Connection Properties command
- Clicking the Data > Connections icon, selecting the desired connection, and clicking the Properties button
- Clicking the properties icon to the right of the connection name field in the External Data Properties dialog box

As you step through the wizard again, you can change your previous selections and launch Microsoft Query.

NOTE

Depending on the complexity of the query, you may receive an alert indicating the query can't be edited with the wizard. Dismissing the alert opens Microsoft Query.

While the Query Wizard provides simple selections, Microsoft Query, pictured in Figure 67 below, provides advanced options for retrieving external data.

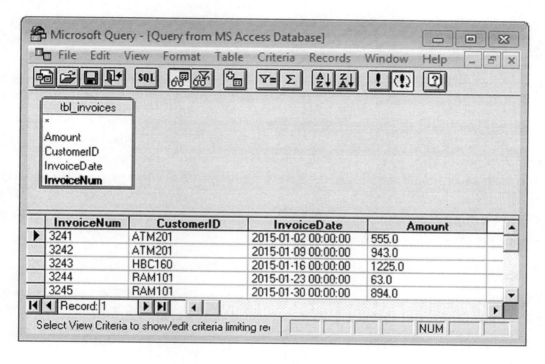

Figure 67

In Microsoft Query you can change the choices made with the wizard and perform advanced tasks not available in the wizard. If you are familiar with the Microsoft Access query designer, you'll feel right at home. You can add, edit, and delete tables and columns used in the query, change the sort order, create filters, view the SQL code, and many other fun things. Although we don't have time to cover these capabilities, I would encourage you to explore them with the Excel help system if this is a feature you'll use in your workbooks.

Can I add a calculated field?

Yes, you can add calculated fields at various points in the data flow, including the data source, Microsoft Query, or the workbook. For example, if the external data source was an Access database, you could add a calculated field to an Access query and then retrieve the Access query into Excel. This is a good option when an administrator wants to control the math from a single location so that the resulting logic is available to all Excel users. You could also place the calculated field inside of Microsoft Query by using the Add Column dialog box to enter the field name and formula. This is a good option when you don't want to worry about formulas inside of your worksheet. You could also place a calculated field within the Excel worksheet, either in the table that stores the external data range or later downstream in the PivotTable or formula-based report. This is a good option when you are most comfortable in Excel and want to be able to easily modify the formula as needed.

Can I aggregate rows?

Yes. Microsoft Query can aggregate the transactions before they are sent to Excel. This is handy when there are many records in the data source but you want fewer rows stored in the Excel file. For example, we could sum the amount column and group the transactions by region, rep, and item by placing the cursor in the amount column and clicking the Sigma button. When you repeatedly click the Sigma button, Excel cycles through various math functions, such as sum, average, and count. Because Excel automatically groups by the remaining columns, be sure to remove any unique identifier columns, such as Transaction ID or other unnecessary columns that could prevent the desired results.

Can I filter rows?

Yes. When source data tables have rows that are not relevant to your current report or workbook, you'll want to set up a filter. You can apply filters at several points along the data flow, including in the data source, Microsoft Query, or the workbook. For example, if the data source was an Access database, you could add a filter to a query and then retrieve the Access query into Excel. This is a good option when a data administrator wants to centrally control the filter rules. You could also add a filter in Microsoft Query by defining one or more criteria. This is a good option when you want to limit the number of rows being stored in the Excel file. Additionally, you could add a filter in Excel, for example by using the numerous PivotTable filtering options previously discussed. This is a good option when you want to be able to quickly change the filter settings in Excel.

Can I store filter criteria values in the worksheet?

Yes. When you define a filter with the Query Wizard, you set the criteria values, and they are used each time you refresh the range. By using a parameter, you can store the criteria values in the worksheet. A parameter tells Excel to ask for the criteria value, which can then be entered or stored in a cell. To set up a parameter within Microsoft Query, simply enclose the user prompt in square brackets and use it as the criteria value. When you refresh the range, Excel will display the Enter Parameter Value dialog box to prompt for the criteria value. For example, the criteria value of *[Please enter the account code]* causes Excel to ask you for the account code. The criteria value can include multiple parameters and comparison operators. For example, if we want the report user to enter the start and end dates for a date field, we could set the criteria value as *Between [Start Date] and [End Date]*. The Enter Parameter Value dialog box allows you to type the value or provide a cell reference. You can also specify the parameter by right-clicking any value cell and selecting the following shortcut menu item:

- Table > Parameters

This discussion sounds similar to our stock quotes exercise from the previous chapter, and indeed, it uses the same underlying parameter feature. We'll get additional parameter practice with an upcoming exercise.

Can I change the external data table name?

Yes. Within Excel, you can change the name of the table that stores the external data by using the Table Tools > Table Name field.

What if the data source moves?

External data connections store absolute paths, so you want to ensure that the external database and tables aren't moved or renamed.

Can I change the table column order in Excel?

Yes. Whether an Excel table is created manually or automatically with the external data feature, you can reposition the column order anytime. Hover the mouse cursor near the column header cell's bottom border and then drag and drop to the desired location.

Can I refresh the data range automatically?

Yes. In addition to manually refreshing the data, you can tell Excel to automatically refresh the range when the workbook is opened or at set intervals while it is open. Both of these options are available in the Usage tab in the Connection Properties dialog box. When a parameter references a cell, you can tell Excel to refresh the range when the cell value is updated. Simply check the Refresh automatically when the cell value changes checkbox in the Enter Parameter Value dialog box.

How can I remove an external data range connection?

Probably the fastest way to remove the external data connection is to right-click any value cell and select:

- Table > Unlink from Data Source

Alternatively, select any value cell and the following Ribbon command:

- TableTools > Design > Convert to Range

How can I get help connecting to my application's database?

Depending on your specific application and network security, you may need to seek assistance from IT staff to connect Excel to the data source. They may be able to install missing drivers, update security permissions, or perform other configuration support.

Once I'm connected to the data source, how do I know which tables to import?

Once you've gained access to the database, it can be time consuming to reverse engineer the database schema, or table structure, and figure out where the desired data is stored. Application developers often create an administrator guide that identifies the tables and fields, so you may want to inquire about obtaining one for your specific application.

What if I want additional information?

Given the variety of data sources and options, connecting to a database can be an involved process. I wanted to provide enough information for you to determine if the topic is relevant and worth pursuing. At a minimum, please note this feature's capabilities in case you encounter a future use for it. For more information, please visit the Excel help system and Microsoft website.

EXAMPLES

Let's practice with some hands-on exercises.

 **PRACTICE**

To work along, please refer to *External Data.xlsx* and the Access database file named *AccessDB.accdb*.

 VIDEO

To watch the solutions video, please visit the Excel University Video Library.

 NOTE

Microsoft Query may not be able to browse inside a ZIP file. If you are working from a ZIP file, please extract the contents before beginning the exercises.

NOTE

The answers file contains the data so that you may compare your results, but I've removed the external data connection. The external data feature stores the database path, and the path on my computer is likely different than on your computer.

 NOTE

If the standard Microsoft Office components are installed on your system, you should be able to complete these exercises without receiving system errors. If you encounter a system error when trying to connect Excel to the Access database, please contact your IT support person for assistance.

EXERCISE 1—FROM ACCESS

In this exercise, we'll retrieve data from an Access database using the From Access command.

PRACTICE

To work along, please refer to the Exercise 1 worksheet.

Our company's chart of accounts is centrally stored in an Access database. We are working on an Excel project and would like to retrieve the chart of accounts. We begin by selecting a worksheet cell to tell Excel where to place the external data. We ensure that the database file is not opened in Access and click the following Ribbon icon:

- Data > From Access

In the resulting Select Data Source dialog box, we browse to the desired Access database *AccessDB. accdb*. Since our database has more than one table, we are prompted by the Select Table dialog box to identify a table within the database.

NOTE

If instead of the Select Table dialog box you receive the Data Link Properties dialog box, it indicates the database file is open in Access. If this happens, dismiss the Data Link Properties dialog box, close the database file, and start over.

From the Select Table dialog, select the *tbl_coa* table and click OK. In the resulting Import Data dialog, we confirm Excel will import the data into a table within an existing worksheet at the cell location we identified previously. Click OK, and bam … the data appears in Excel. Next period we refresh the range to retrieve the current chart of accounts.

While this method makes it easy to retrieve data, it does not provide the full capabilities of the external data feature and can create file locks that hamper productivity, especially in multi-user environments. In the next exercise, we'll use my preferred method, Microsoft Query.

EXERCISE 2—MS QUERY

Let's use Microsoft Query to retrieve data from an Access database.

 **PRACTICE**

To work along, please refer to the Exercise 2 worksheet.

Our employee data is stored in an Access database, and we need to pull it into Excel for analysis. We select a worksheet cell so Excel knows where to place the data and click the following Ribbon icon:

- Data > From Other Sources > From Microsoft Query

In the Choose Data Source dialog box, we double-click MS Access Database. In the resulting Select Database dialog box, we browse to the drive and directory that has our database and double-click the database name *AccessDB.accdb*. This launches the Query Wizard. The first step asks us to identify the table and columns, so we select the *tbl_employees* table and click the Right Arrow button to select all columns. The next step asks us to identify the desired rows, and since we want all rows, we proceed without defining any filters. The next step allows us to specify a sort order, and because we aren't concerned about sort order, we proceed to the next step. The final step allows us to return the data to Excel or further edit the query. Our query was simple enough to be fully defined with the wizard, so we return the data to Excel. In the resulting Import Data dialog box, we confirm the data will be imported into a table at the location of our previously selected cell. We click OK, and bam … the data pours into our worksheet.

To update the external data range next period, we don't need to go through the wizard again. We simply use the refresh command. Let's check it out. We delete the imported worksheet rows for employee numbers 11 and higher. With these worksheet rows gone, the table only includes employee numbers 1 through 10. We click the Refresh button and watch the records flow in, almost as if by magic.

EXERCISE 3—REPORT FEED

In this exercise, we'll build reports based on an external data range.

 **PRACTICE**

To work along, please refer to the Exercise 3 worksheet.

Our company stores sales data in an Access database, and we need to build a summary report by region based on that data. We begin by getting the data into our workbook. We use Microsoft Query to retrieve all columns and rows from the *tbl_sales* table stored in the *AccessDB.accdb* database.

With the data in Excel, it is time to build our summary report. Since we'll summarize the data in the worksheet table, we inspect the table name. The default table name is pretty funky, something like *Table_Query_from_MS_Access_Database*. Although we could rename the table, we'll stick with the default, and keep moving. Just for fun, let's build a formula-based report and a PivotTable.

Starting with the formula report, we generate and sort a unique list of region labels, and use our friend SUMIFS to generate the values. Toss in skinny and total rows for good measure, and we're done.

For the PivotTable version, we build the following report:

- PT ROWS: Region; VALUES: Sum(Amount)

Hey, that was easy. Next period, we can simply refresh the data range to retrieve any updated records from the database. Since we used the table name to build our reports, any new transactions will be included when we refresh the external data ... or will they? It depends on whether or not the new transactions include any new regions. The PivotTable will include all transactions because it dynamically expands to incorporate any new regions.

Note that the formula-based report will not reflect all transactions if new regions appear. In a formula-based report, we would need to manually add report labels for any new regions and fill the formulas down. The inclusion of new items is a key difference between the two report types, which we previously explored. By the way, regarding our formula-based report, how can we be notified when new regions are added? If we assume that the total of the external data will not agree with the report total when new regions appear in the data, we can easily set up a related test on an error check sheet.

 XREF

The inclusion of new items is discussed in Chapter 11: Report Type Comparison. Setting up an error check sheet is discussed in Volume 2, Chapter 25.

EXERCISE 4—PIVOTTABLE DIRECT

In this exercise, we'll send external data directly to a PivotTable.

 **PRACTICE**

To work along, please refer to the Exercise 4 worksheet.

We need to summarize the data stored in an Access database. Rather than retrieve the data and place it into a table, as we did in the previous exercise, we'll place it directly into a PivotTable.

Using Microsoft Query, we walk through the wizard to retrieve all columns and rows from the *tbl_ checks* table stored in the *AccessDB.accdb* database. When we get to the Import Data dialog, we select PivotTable Report and click OK. We see the familiar PivotTable interface and PivotTable Field list, but the data does not appear in the worksheet. Although this feels weird, we simply build the PivotTable as we've done many times before. We create the following report:

- PT ROWS: VID; VALUES: Sum(Amount)

This PivotTable is linked to the external data source. When we refresh the PivotTable, Excel updates the PivotTable cache by refreshing the external data range. We can interact with the PivotTable as normal, including sorting, filtering, and drilling down.

EXERCISE 5—PARAMETER QUERY

In this exercise, we'll set up a parameter query so that we can retrieve external data based on criteria values stored in the worksheet.

 **PRACTICE**

To work along, please refer to the Exercise 5 worksheet.

The accounting data is stored in the *AccessDB.accdb* database, and we need to retrieve the invoice transactions from the *tbl_invoices* table. Rather than retrieve all transactions, we want to obtain the transactions that fall within a date range specified in our worksheet. The date range will be stored in two worksheet cells. One will store the start date, and the other will store the end date.

We walk through the steps of the Query Wizard to identify the database, table, columns, and rows, and when we get to the final step, we choose to edit the query in Microsoft Query.

NOTE

Setting up a parameter would be easier if we could use the wizard's filter step, but to my knowledge this option is not available.

With Microsoft Query open, let's set up the start and end date parameters. If the criteria pane is not displayed, we toggle it on by selecting the following menu item:

- View > Criteria

 NOTE

If we had defined any filters in the wizard, we would see them in the criteria pane.

To establish a filter, we use the criteria pane to specify the criteria field and the criteria value. In our case, we want to limit the rows retrieved to the transactions dated on or between our start and end dates. We select the ***InvoiceDate*** field from the criteria field drop-down. Although we could enter a date as a criteria value, we want to have Microsoft Query obtain the criteria values from the Excel worksheet. By using a parameter for the criteria value, we instruct Excel to ask the user for the value. Because our query actually needs to retrieve transactions dated between two dates, inclusive, we set up two parameters, as follows:

```
Between [Please enter starting date] and [Please enter
ending date]
```

Please note the elegant between/and syntax, which is an alternative to using comparison operators such as >=. Microsoft Query supports sophisticated criteria settings, including and/or logic, constants, comparison operators, and wildcards. Please use the Microsoft Query help system for related syntax and more information. The parameter text placed between the square brackets represents the message to the user. We could also have used the following criteria value:

```
Between [Start date?] and [End date?]
```

Or my personal favorite:

```
Between [StartDate] and [EndDate]
```

When we are satisfied with our criteria value, we return to Excel by clicking the return data icon or selecting the following menu item:

- File > Return data to Microsoft Excel

When prompted by Excel to provide the start and end dates, we enter them. The dates we enter at this point simply allow Microsoft Query to move forward and aren't stored permanently. Once we arrive back in Excel, we see the familiar Import Data dialog box. We opt to return the data to a table, and bam, the data appears in our worksheet.

The final step is to tell Excel to use the input cell values for the start and end dates. If we refresh the range, Excel displays the Enter Parameter Value dialog box for each parameter and allows us to reference the input cell.

 NOTE

Excel supports A1-style parameter cell references, but to my knowledge not named references.

We can also check the Use this value/reference for future refreshes checkbox so that Excel remembers this choice next time.

 NOTE

If we check the Refresh automatically when cell value changes checkbox, then Excel will retrieve data when we enter a different value into the input cell.

If needed, we can edit the parameter settings at any time with the Parameters dialog box by right-clicking a table cell and selecting the following shortcut menu item:

- Table > Parameters

To edit a parameter setting, select the desired parameter name from the list box and then choose the appropriate radio button on the right. After telling Excel to obtain the parameter values from the input cells, we can simply change the start and end dates in the worksheet and refresh.

This ability to easily retrieve a specific range of transactions can create significant efficiency gains. We simply enter the start and end dates to specify any date range and then click the Refresh button to retrieve the related transactions.

EXERCISE 6—V2 REVISITED

In this exercise, we'll apply the external data feature to optimize a familiar report.

 **PRACTICE**

To work along, please refer to the Exercise 6 worksheet.

Let's revisit a report that we've built twice already. We first built the report at the end of Volume 2. Our approach was to paste the exported data into a worksheet, store it in a table, generate the report labels, and compute the report values with formulas. The second time we built it was in this volume, Chapter 11: Report Type Comparison, where our approach shifted. We pasted the data into a worksheet, stored it in a table, and created a PivotTable instead of a formula-based report. This time, we will use the external data feature to retrieve and send the data directly into a PivotTable. I'm giddy with anticipation.

The data is stored in the *tbl_transactions* table of the *AccessDB.accdb* database. We walk through the Query Wizard and pick the database, table, all columns, and all rows. When we get the Import Data dialog box, we opt to return the data to a PivotTable report.

 NOTE

To my knowledge, Excel doesn't support parameters when sending external data directly to a PivotTable.

When we see the familiar PivotTable interface, we use it to create the following report:

- PT ROWS: Account; COLUMNS: Month(Date); VALUES: Sum(Amount); FILTERS: Year(Date), Department

Wow, it worked! In future periods, we simply refresh the PivotTable, and Excel then retrieves any updated or new records from the external data source and summarizes them in the report. Updating this report requires a single click. And that, my friend, is how we can minimize the time it takes to update this recurring-use report.

CHAPTER CONCLUSION

This chapter provided an overview of the external data feature and an opportunity for hands-on practice. I've tried to keep the chapter short in case the feature isn't relevant to your work. If it is relevant, I hope this chapter provided enough information for you to get started. As you can tell, there are many details and capabilities worth exploring, especially when you want to eliminate manual steps from recurring processes. Please reference the built-in Excel help system for more information.

Authentication

Chapter 23: Text Files

Efficiency

SET UP

Sometimes the data we want to summarize is stored in a text file. Although applications often support exporting data to an Excel file, there are many accounting systems, databases, and websites that provide data in text files. Fortunately, Excel is proficient at opening text files and provides several tools for working with them.

Let's distinguish a file extension from a file format. Generally the file extension indicates the file format, for example, CSV and TXT extensions indicate a text format. Text files come in a variety of extensions. Although Windows allows you to rename a file as well as change the extension, doing so does not change the file format.

Since a file's extension usually indicates the format, Windows associates file extensions with a default application. For example, XLSX files are automatically opened with Excel. Often several different applications can open files of a given extension or type. For example, Notepad, Wordpad, and Excel can all open text files.

In practice you may encounter a program that is unable to export to an Excel file. If so, don't give up. You may find it is able to export a report or transaction listing as a text file, and even if it assigns an unfamiliar extension, such as EXP, you can likely open it with Excel.

HOW TO

There are several ways to get text data into Excel. We'll explore the following methods:

- Open a text file

- Import with external data

- Copy/Paste

Each method enables us to get text data into Excel, and we can select which to use based on the data source.

OPEN A TEXT FILE

One way to open a computer file is to double-click it within a file explorer such as Windows Explorer. This approach opens the file with the application associated with its extension. You can also open a file from within a specific application. Since Excel usually isn't associated with most text file extensions, you'll want to first open Excel and then open the text file.

From Excel's perspective, text files are either delimited or fixed width. Delimited files identify content regions, such as fields or columns, with designated characters. A famous delimiter is a comma. Files delimited with commas have been assigned a specific extension, CSV, which stands for Comma Separated Values. Excel easily opens CSV files and is often the associated application for them. Excel can also open files delimited with other characters, such as dashes or semicolons. For Excel, a file without delimiters is referred to as fixed width. Since Excel can't always automatically determine the column breaks, we can manually assign them.

Let's walk through an example. Before we open the text file in Excel, let's first open it with a text editor such as Notepad so we can see the contents, as shown in Figure 68 below.

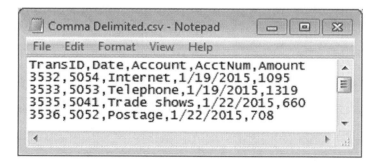

Figure 68

We observe that commas separate the columns, and the first line represents column headers. We close the file and launch Excel. We ask Excel to open a file and receive the standard File Open dialog box. The dialog automatically filters the folder contents and only displays files with valid Excel extensions, such as XLSX. Although this helps ensure we only open valid Excel files, it prevents us from seeing all files, including text files. Fortunately, we can easily remedy this and view all files. In the dialog box we change the filter option from the current setting, such as All Excel Files, to All Files. Now that we can see all files, we select the desired text file. Since our file happened to be a CSV file, Excel opens it immediately.

Now, let's take a look at another text file in Notepad, shown in Figure 69 below.

Figure 69

When we try to open this file in Excel, we are greeted with the Text Import Wizard. The first step asks if the file is delimited or fixed width and if the data has headers. Were we to select the Delimited option, Excel would ask us to identify the delimiter, such as comma, tab, colon, or other. Since our file has no delimiter, we select the fixed width option. In the next step, we manually define the column breaks. When we click the preview pane, Excel inserts a vertical line that represents a column break. We continue adding, moving, or removing column breaks until they are positioned as desired. In the final step of the wizard, we can specify data types for the columns if desired. When we complete the wizard, we see that the text file has opened in Excel. We can now edit the data or save the file as an Excel file type. Better yet, we can copy/paste the transactions into a table in a reporting workbook. Since the table will auto-expand, the transactions will automatically flow into the report.

◉ NOTE

This text wizard will become familiar because Excel uses it to complete various tasks, including opening text files, retrieving external data from text files, and converting text to columns.

IMPORT WITH EXTERNAL DATA

The external data feature also can be used to retrieve text file data. This approach basically combines the external data process with the Text Import Wizard. After selecting the desired destination cell, we click the following Ribbon icon:

- Data > From Text

We'll be asked to identify the text file and walk through the Text Import Wizard. This process creates a refreshable range and saves us from having to repeat the copy/paste step each time we want to update the workbook. When importing a consistently structured text file on a recurring basis, this option is definitely worth exploring.

COPY/PASTE

When we can't get the data we need into a text file, our only option may be to copy/paste. For example, we may need to copy data from an application window, an on-screen report, a website, or a PDF file. When we copy multiple data columns, Excel often recognizes them and places the data into corresponding worksheet columns. Sometimes however, Excel pastes multiple data columns into a single worksheet column. When it does, we can use the Convert Text to Columns Wizard to split the column into multiple columns based on a delimited or fixed width format.

 NOTE

The FlashFill feature introduced with Excel 2013 provides an alternative to the Convert Text to Columns Wizard.

To split a single column into multiple columns, select the data in the column and then the following Ribbon command:

- Data > Text to Columns

You'll be presented with a familiar text wizard. Complete the steps to split the single column into multiple columns.

NOTE

This feature can also be used to convert a column's data type. Select the desired data type in the final step of the wizard.

EXAMPLES

Let's practice with a few hands-on exercises.

 **PRACTICE**

To work along, please refer to *Text Files.xlsx.*

 VIDEO

To watch the solutions video, please visit the Excel University Video Library.

EXERCISE 1—COMMA DELIMITED

In this exercise, we'll add the transactions in a text file to our reporting workbook.

 **PRACTICE**

To work along, please refer to the Exercise 1 worksheet.

We already have set up our reporting workbook. The data is stored in the *tbl_e1_data* table on the *E1 Data* worksheet, and the formula-based report is on the *Exercise 1* worksheet.

This period we need to update the report by including the transactions stored in a text file. From within Excel, we open the *Comma Delimited.csv* file. We copy the data, excluding the header row, and append it to our *tbl_e1_data* table with a standard paste. The table auto-expands to include the new transactions, and we confirm they flow into the report as expected.

EXERCISE 2—FIXED WIDTH

In this exercise, we'll grab data from a fixed width text file.

 **PRACTICE**

To work along, please refer to the Exercise 2 worksheet.

Similar to the previous exercise, we need to update our reporting workbook with transactions stored in a text file. The data is stored in the *tbl_e2_data* table on the *E2 Data* sheet, and the formula-based report is on the *Exercise 2* sheet.

This period, we need to update the report by including the transactions stored in a text file. From within Excel, we open the *Fixed Width.txt* file. Oh, hello text wizard. Excel needs help figuring out where to place the columns. In the first step, we tell Excel that our file is fixed width. Next, we use the data preview pane to manually set the column breaks. To add a new column break, we click the data preview pane. To edit a column break, we click and drag it to the desired position. To remove a column break, we double-click it. Once our column breaks look good, we proceed to the final step. At this step, we could define the data type for each column and specify advanced settings, but the defaults are fine, so we just click Finish.

Excel is now able to open the file and display the data. We copy the transactions and paste-append them to our *tbl_e2_data* table. The table auto-expands, and the data flows into our report. Mission accomplished.

EXERCISE 3—OTHER DELIMITER

In this exercise, we'll open a delimited text file.

 **PRACTICE**

To work along, please refer to the Exercise 3 worksheet.

We store a list of accounts in a worksheet to use as needed. We've recently added some accounts to our accounting system, so we export an updated list to a text file named *Delimited.txt*. We'd like to replace our Excel list with the accounts in the text file.

We begin by opening the text file from within Excel and are presented with the familiar text wizard. In the first step, we tell Excel that the file is delimited. In the next step, we observe the data preview window and can easily see that the delimiter is a colon. Excel, however, doesn't know what the delimiter is and presents all data in a single column. Because the colon isn't a built-in choice, we define the delimiter for Excel by checking the Other checkbox and entering a colon. Bam. The preview window updates, and the data snaps into separate columns. We finish the wizard and view the file in Excel. We copy the account list and paste it into the table to replace the existing accounts.

EXERCISE 4—EXTERNAL DATA

In this exercise, we'll use the external data feature to retrieve data from a text file.

 **PRACTICE**

To work along, please refer to the Exercise 4 worksheet.

The *Delimited.txt* file has the data we need to import. Rather than asking Excel to open the text file, we'll ask it to import the file's contents. After selecting the desired cell location in our worksheet, we click the following Ribbon icon:

- Data > From Text

We select the text file and are greeted with the familiar text wizard. We quickly work through the wizard, letting Excel know that the file is delimited with a colon. When we complete the wizard, Excel displays the Import Data dialog box. We confirm the cell reference and click OK.

This process has retrieved the data from the text file and stored it in a named, refreshable range. When we click the Refresh button, Excel asks us to confirm the file and then retrieves its contents. Since Excel remembers our previous delimiter selection, it doesn't display the Text Import Wizard. We can reference the data range with its name as needed.

EXERCISE 5—TEXT TO COLUMNS

In this exercise, we'll use the Convert Text to Columns Wizard to split data into multiple columns.

 **PRACTICE**

To work along, please refer to the Exercise 5 worksheet.

The **Delimited.pdf** file contains data we need to bring into Excel. We open it with our default PDF reader application, such as Adobe Reader. We copy the data from the PDF file and paste it into our Excel worksheet. Since the data came into a single column, we need to split it into multiple columns. We select the data range and the following Ribbon command:

- Data > Text to Columns

We are greeted with the familiar text wizard. We walk through it and let Excel know the text is delimited with a colon. Excel splits the data into multiple columns and removes the colons.

 NOTE

The copy/paste method works fine for small PDF tables. When the data is more complex or spans multiple pages, you may want to explore the tools in the full version of Adobe Acrobat or a third-party utility.

CHAPTER CONCLUSION

This chapter explored several ways to get text data into Excel. In practice, these techniques come in handy when data is delivered in text format.

Chapter 24: Data Preparation

efficiency

SET UP

A common process used to exchange data between computer systems, applications, or databases is to extract data from the source system, transform it into the desired format, and load it into the target system. This common process even has its own acronym, ETL, which is short for extract, transform, and load. Applying this concept to our Excel reporting workbooks will help us see and optimize the entire data flow and identify the features, functions, and techniques that can efficiently accomplish each task.

Consider the reporting workbooks we've created together. We have frequently taken data exported from an accounting system and loaded it into a PivotTable report. Since we've already explored the extract and load tasks by examining ways to get and summarize external data, this chapter focuses on the transformation step and discusses efficient ways to prepare data for our reports.

What are examples of transformations? The following common tasks help prepare exported data for reporting purposes:

- Include only certain columns
- Include only certain rows
- Aggregate rows
- Transpose values
- Sort the data
- Derive a calculated value

- Translate coded values

- Join multiple columns into a single column

- Split a column into multiple columns

- Flatten data

Fortunately, PivotTables automatically handle several of these tasks. Can you identify which ones? We include certain columns by inserting selected fields into the report. We include certain rows by using field filters, report filters, or slicers. PivotTables automatically aggregate rows and generate subtotals for row fields. PivotTables transpose values when we move fields between the row and column layout areas. A PivotTable report can be sorted ascending, descending, or manually. As you can see, PivotTables easily perform the first five transformation tasks. Since we've already discussed the mechanics of each at length, let's tackle the remaining tasks in the list.

HOW TO

We'll explore ways to efficiently address each of the following tasks:

- Derive a calculated value

- Translate coded values

- Join multiple columns

- Split a column

- Flatten data

DERIVE A CALCULATED VALUE

When a column needed for reporting purposes doesn't exist in the data source, we'll use a formula to create a calculated field. For example, the source data may include a sales amount column but not a commission column. We can derive the commission amount with a formula. In addition to numeric values, calculated fields can return other data types, such as dates or text strings, which may be useful. For example, we can use a calculated field to create report groups such as fiscal period groups.

We previously created calculated fields with PivotTable formulas. Another option, which often provides more power and flexibility, is to create the calculated field with a formula in the data table. With this approach, we are free to write formulas without the restrictions imposed by PivotTable formulas. If we keep the calculated field or fields to the right of the extracted data, the table is easy to maintain. We paste the new transactions into the table, and it fills the calculated fields down.

 XREF

Placing a calculated field in a PivotTable is discussed in Chapter 15: Calculated Fields.

We can use the same technique to perform other transformations as well, such as translating values.

TRANSLATE CODED VALUES

When the extracted data labels are different than the labels required for reporting purposes, we'll need to translate them. For example, the extract may provide account codes or numbers, but the report needs to reflect account names. To retain the original data structure, we'll add a calculated field to perform the translation. In future periods, we paste transactions into the table, and the calculated field automatically performs the translation.

In practice, we can store a translation table in the workbook, for example a chart of accounts. This makes it easy to convert account numbers to names. The translation formula can incorporate functions such as VLOOKUP, INDEX, and MATCH or any others needed to retrieve or derive the desired label.

JOIN MULTIPLE COLUMNS

When the exported data delivers values in multiple columns that need to be combined for reporting purposes, we may need to join them. For example, the extract stores the account and subaccount in individual columns, but our report needs to present the combined full account. Again, we'll add a new calculated field in the table. Can you think of a function we could use to join text values? Come on, be there for me. Yes, CONCATENATE. With this function, it is easy to write a formula that combines the account and subaccount values for reporting purposes.

 XREF

The CONCATENATE function is discussed in Volume 2, Chapter 19.

SPLIT A COLUMN

When the exported data delivers values in a single column that need to be separate for reporting purposes, we may need to split the values into multiple columns. For example, the extract includes a column that combines the department and account numbers, but we need to group the report by department. There are a variety of ways to split a column into its constituent parts.

Can you think of a feature we could use to split a column? Yes, the text to columns feature can perform this task. If this were a one-time project, using this manual feature would probably be just fine. However we try to eliminate manual steps from recurring processes. Rather than use this feature, we'll use formulas, because calculated fields in tables automatically fill down when we add new transactions. The following five handy text functions can help with this task:

- LEFT—returns a given number of characters from the left side of a text string

- RIGHT—returns a given number of characters from the right side of a text string

- MID—returns a given number of characters from the middle of a text string

- FIND—returns the position of the matching character in a text string

- LEN—returns the length of a text string

Let's explore them one at a time.

LEFT

The LEFT function returns a specified number of characters from the beginning of a text string. The syntax follows:

```
=LEFT(text,[num_chars])
```

Where:

- **text** is the text string containing the characters to return

- **[num_chars]** is the optional number of characters to return; defaults to one if omitted

Let's say column *A* stores full account codes. Our full account codes have two segments, the department number and the account number. Since our report needs to group transactions by department, we'll create a calculated column for the department number. If *A1* contained the full account code 101-3056, we use the following formula to retrieve the department number 101:

```
=LEFT(A1,3)
```

Where:

- **A1** is the full account code

- **3** is the number of characters to return

Assuming all department numbers are three characters, this formula can be filled down to create the department column.

 NOTE

Since the LEFT function operates on the stored value rather than the displayed value, it disregards any formatting, such as a leading currency symbol.

RIGHT

The RIGHT function is similar to the LEFT function, except it retrieves characters from the end of the string. The syntax follows:

```
=RIGHT(text,[num_chars])
```

Where:

- **text** is the text string containing the characters to return

- **[num_chars]** is the optional number of characters to return; defaults to one if omitted

Let's say column *A* stores full account codes. Our full account codes have two segments, the department number and the account number. Since our report needs to group transactions by account, we will create a calculated column for the account number. Assuming *A1* has the full account code 101-3056, we use the following formula to retrieve the account number 3056:

```
=RIGHT(A1,4)
```

Where:

- **A1** is the full account code

- **4** is the number of characters to return

Assuming all account numbers are four characters, this formula can be filled down to create the account column.

MID

The MID function retrieves characters from the middle of a text string. The syntax follows:

```
=MID(text,start_num,num_chars)
```

Where:

- **text** is the text string containing the characters to return
- **start_num** is the starting character position
- **num_chars** is the number of characters to return

Let's say column *A* stores full product codes. Our product codes have three segments: category, item code, and option. Since our report needs to group transactions by item code, we will create a calculated field for it. If *A1* has a product code of 700-E660-A, we could use the following formula to return E660:

```
=MID(A1,5,4)
```

Where:

- **A1** is the full product code
- **5** is the starting character position
- **4** is the number of characters

Assuming all item codes begin at the fifth position and contain four characters, this formula can be filled down to create the item code column. But what if all item codes aren't four characters? Hmmm.

The LEFT, RIGHT, and MID examples above assumed codes were uniform in length, for example, all department numbers were three digits, and all account numbers were four digits. In practice this uniformity may not be the case, and we may need to write formulas that accommodate variable-length strings. In these cases, we can incorporate the FIND function to locate the delimiter.

 NOTE

LEFT, RIGHT, and MID return a text string, not a numeric value. If you need to convert the result into a numeric value, which function can help? Yes, the VALUE function.

XREF

The VALUE function is discussed in Volume 2, chapter 7.

FIND

The FIND function enables us to write formulas that accommodate variable-length strings by locating the delimiter and passing its location to the LEFT, RIGHT, or MID function. The FIND function locates a character within a text string and returns its position number. Does this remind you of any other functions? Yes, the MATCH function, which returns the relative position of a list item. The MATCH function operates on worksheet cells, whereas the FIND function operates in a text string.

 XREF

The MATCH function is discussed in Volume 2, Chapter 6.

I think about the FIND function in these terms: *find this, in here.* The syntax follows:

```
=FIND(find_text,within_text,[start_num])
```

Where:

- **find_text** is the character or string you are seeking
- **within_text** is the text string in which you are looking
- **[start_num]** is the optional position at which to start the search; defaults to one if omitted

 NOTE

If FIND can't locate the character it is seeking, it returns #VALUE!.

If cell *A1* contained the full account code 101-3056, we could use the following formula to return the position of the dash delimiter:

```
=FIND("-",A1,1)
```

Where:

- **"-"** is the delimiter we are seeking

- **A1** is the full account code

- **1** tells the function to start at the first character

Now that we have the position of the dash delimiter, we can return the characters before it with the LEFT function. For example, if **A1** contained the full account code 101-3056, we could use the following formula to return department 101:

```
=LEFT(A1, FIND("-",A1,1)-1)
```

Where:

- **A1** is the full account code

- **FIND("-", A1, 1)-1** returns the position of the dash, minus one

- **Where:**

    o **"-"** is the delimiter

    o **A1** is the full account code

    o **1** tells the function to start at the first character

- **-1** subtracts one to exclude the final character from the result, in this case a dash

The formula evaluation sequence follows:

```
=LEFT(A1,FIND("-", A1, 1)-1)
=LEFT(A1,4-1)
=LEFT(A1,3)
="101"
```

Since the formula returns the characters to the left of the dash, it easily accommodates variable-length department numbers as it is filled through the range.

Let's try to use the FIND function with the RIGHT function to retrieve the account number from a full account code. For example, let's say **A1** contains the full account code 1015-305, where 1015 is the department number, and 305 is the account number. Unfortunately, we can't simply use FIND as the second argument of the RIGHT function, as illustrated by the following formula. Instead of returning the desired result of 305, the formula would return 5-305:

```
=RIGHT(A1,FIND("-",A1,1))
```

Where:

- **A1** is the full account code

- **FIND("-",A1,1)** returns the position of the dash

The formula evaluation sequence follows:

```
=RIGHT(A1,FIND("-",A1,1))

=RIGHT(A1,5)

="5-305"
```

The formula returns 5-305 rather than the desired result of 305 because the FIND function searches from the left and returns 5 to the RIGHT function. Since the FIND function searches from the left, it is easily nested into the LEFT function. To use FIND with the RIGHT function, FIND would need to search from the right. Since we can't tell the FIND function to search from the right, we'll need another way to compute the number of characters to the right of the delimiter. Fortunately, we can accomplish this with simple subtraction.

When we count the total number of characters in the text string 1015-305, we get 8. The position of the dash is 5. If we subtract the total 8 from the position of the dash 5, we get the number of characters to the right of the dash, which is 3. Since we already know how to determine the position of the dash with the FIND function, let's discuss LEN, which counts the number of characters in a text string.

 NOTE

In addition to the FIND function, which is case sensitive, you can use the SEARCH function, which is not case sensitive.

LEN

The LEN function returns the length of a text string. The syntax follows:

```
=LEN(text)
```

Where:

- **text** is the text string

Let's say column **A** stores full account codes. Our full account codes have two variable-length segments, the department number and the account number. Since our report needs to group transactions by account, we will create a calculated column for the account number. Assuming *A1* contains the full account code 1015-305, we will use the following formula to return the account number 305:

```
=RIGHT(A1,LEN(A1)-FIND("-",A1,1))
```

Where:

- **A1** is the full account code
- **LEN(A1)** returns the number of characters
- **Where:**
    - **A1** is the full account code
- **FIND("-",A1,1)** returns the position of the dash
- **Where:**
    - **"-"** is the character we are seeking
    - **A1** is where we are looking
    - **1** tells the function to start at the first character

The formula evaluation sequence follows:

```
=RIGHT(A1,LEN(A1)-FIND("-",A1,1))
=RIGHT(A1,8-FIND("-",A1,1))
=RIGHT(A1,8-5))
=RIGHT(A1,3)
="305"
```

The five functions discussed above can be used together to help split text strings with formulas.

 NOTE

If your text string contains multiple delimiters, FIND easily locates the first one because it searches from the left. However, because FIND doesn't search from the right, it is not as easy to locate the final delimiter. The Excel University blog post "Find the Last Occurrence of a Delimiter to Retrieve the Lowest Sub Account from QuickBooks in Excel" illustrates one approach to locating the final delimiter.

FLATTEN DATA

Because Excel is best equipped to summarize data that is in a flat format, we may need to flatten exported data. We previously discussed the characteristics of flat data, but, in summary, flat data repeats labels as needed so that all information about a record is stored in a row.

 XREF

> Flat data is discussed in Volume 1, Chapter 16.

We can quickly flatten data with the following manual technique:

1. Select the label range—select the cells with the labels you want to repeat

2. Reselect blank cells only—update the current selection to include blank cells only

3. Formula—write a formula that retrieves the value from the cell above

4. Paste values—copy and paste values to replace the formulas with values

Let's work through the steps using the exported data illustrated in Figure 70 below.

	B	C	D	E
9	**Name**	**Account**	**Date**	**Amount**
10	Bayshore Water	Fuel	4/28/2015	24.00
11			5/5/2015	24.50
12			5/12/2015	25.00
13		Utilities	5/12/2015	38.75
14	Cal Gas & Electric	Office expenses	1/21/2015	156.22
15			2/25/2015	122.51
16			3/24/2015	113.89

Figure 70

 XREF

> This technique, which I first saw in John Walkenbach's excellent book *Excel 2007 Formulas*, was noted in Volume 2, Chapter 3. Thanks John!

Select the Label Range

Select the range of labels you want to repeat or fill down, such as the report labels found in columns **B** and **C** in the screenshot above. Exclude data cells that are already flat.

Reselect Blank Cells Only

Before you write the formula to repeat the labels, you want to include only blank cells in your selection. Fortunately, Excel provides an easy way to do this with the Go To Special dialog box. You can open the dialog with the following Ribbon command:

- Home > Find & Select > Go To Special…

[handwritten notes: A = All (Select any) B = blanks (go to special) C = cell above (= up one) D = down — ctl enter]

I prefer to open this dialog by pressing F5 to open the Go To dialog box, and Alt+S to select the Special button.

The Go To Special dialog provides many fun options you'll want to explore. For this task, select **Blanks** and click OK. The selection is updated to only include the blank cells within the original range.

When the Go To Special command is executed, the active selection determines the scope of operation. If a single cell is selected, the command operates on the used cells in the sheet. If a range is selected, the command operates within the selected range.

Formula

The next step is to write a formula in all blank cells that retrieves the value from the cell above. Type an equal sign into the active cell and tap the Up Arrow key. You want to fill this formula into all selected cells. Do you remember how? Yes, by hitting Ctrl+Enter instead of Enter. *[handwritten notes: fill down]*

Ctrl+Enter is discussed in Volume 1, Chapter 18.

Bam. The formula is filled into all selected cells, effectively repeating the labels and flattening the data.

Paste Values

The final step is to replace the formulas with values. Select the entire label range, not just the formula cells, and do a standard copy. Then paste the values to replace the formulas with values.

NOTE

There are several ways to paste values, such as right-clicking and selecting values from the shortcut menu, using the Paste Special dialog box and selecting the values option, or selecting the following Ribbon command:

- Home > Paste > Values

 NOTE

As a general practice, and especially when pasting between workbooks, it is cleaner to paste values because a standard paste may bring in unwanted attributes, such as names, external cell references, and formats.

Our worksheet now includes flat data, as shown in Figure 71 below.

	B	C	D	E
9	**Name**	**Account**	**Date**	**Amount**
10	Bayshore Water	Fuel	4/28/2015	24.00
11	Bayshore Water	Fuel	5/5/2015	24.50
12	Bayshore Water	Fuel	5/12/2015	25.00
13	Bayshore Water	Utilities	5/12/2015	38.75
14	Cal Gas & Electric	Office expenses	1/21/2015	156.22
15	Cal Gas & Electric	Office expenses	2/25/2015	122.51
16	Cal Gas & Electric	Office expenses	3/24/2015	113.89

Figure 71

Ready to practice by working through the exercises? I packed the workbook full of extra credit exercises for you, so please don't miss out on the fun!

EXAMPLES

Let's crack open the exercise workbook and practice several data transformations.

 **PRACTICE**

To work along, please refer to *Data Preparation.xlsx.*

 VIDEO

To watch the solutions video, please visit the Excel University Video Library.

EXERCISE 1—CALCULATED FIELD

Let's revisit an exercise and solve it in a new way. Previously we built a PivotTable that included multiple value fields. In order to reflect a total of the value fields in the report, we used a PivotTable formula to create a calculated field.

 XREF

Using a PivotTable formula to create a calculated field is discussed in Chapter 15: Calculated Fields.

In this exercise, we'll create the calculated field in the data source table. In practice this is my preferred approach.

 **PRACTICE**

To work along, please refer to the Exercise 1 worksheet.

The exported data is stored on the *E1 Data* sheet in the *tbl_e1_data* table and contains InvoiceNum, Data, Customer, Amount, SalesTax, and Shipping columns. We want to summarize the transactions by customer and provide amount, sales tax, shipping, and total columns. Since the exported data does not contain a total column, we'll add a calculated field to the data table.

We enter the new column header, Total, and the table auto-expands to the right. There are two ways to write the formula that adds the amount, sales tax, and shipping columns. We could use the addition operator with individual column references or a summing function with a multicolumn range reference. For example, we could use the addition operator with individual column references as illustrated in the following formula:

```
=[@Amount]+[@SalesTax]+[@Shipping]
```

In this approach, any new columns inserted into the data table are excluded from this total. Depending on the circumstances, this may or may not be desired. We could instead use a summing function with a multicolumn range reference, as illustrated in the following formula:

```
=SUM(tbl_e1_data[@[Amount]:[Shipping]])
```

In this approach, any new columns inserted between these columns are included in the total. Depending on the circumstances, this may or may not be desired.

XREF

Structured table range references are discussed in Chapter 14: Multiple Value Fields.

Since we don't expect any new columns to be inserted in future periods, either approach works just fine. Once the calculated field is in the table, it is easy to summarize the transactions with the following report:

- PT ROWS: Customer; VALUES: Sum(Amount), Sum(SalesTax), Sum(Shipping), Sum(Total)

We complete the report by formatting the value fields.

EXERCISE 2—ACCOUNT NAMES

In this exercise, we'll translate coded values.

PRACTICE

To work along, please refer to the Exercise 2 worksheet.

The exported data is stored in the *tbl_e2_data* table on the *E2 Data* sheet and contains TransID, Date, AcctNum, and Amount columns. Since our report must include account names, even though the data doesn't, we'll set up a calculated field to translate account numbers to names. We store the chart of accounts in a table named *tbl_coa* so that we can easily perform the translation with a lookup formula.

We enter the new column header, AcctName, and the table auto-expands to the right. We retrieve the account name from the chart of accounts with the following lookup formula:

```
=VLOOKUP([@AcctNum],tbl_coa,2,0)
```

Where:

- **[@AcctNum]** is the lookup value, the account number

- **tbl_coa** is the lookup range, the chart of accounts

- **2** is the return column, the account name column

- **0** means exact match

Once the calculated field is in the table, we can easily summarize the transactions with the following report:

- PT ROWS: AcctNum, AcctName; VALUES: Sum(Amount)

We complete the report by changing the layout to tabular, removing subtotals for the AcctNum field, and formatting the value fields.

EXERCISE 3—FISCAL QUARTERS

In this exercise, we'll use a calculated field for report groups and subtotals.

 **PRACTICE**

To work along, please refer to the Exercise 3 worksheet.

The exported data is stored in the *tbl_e3_data* table on the *E3 Data* sheet and contains TransID, Date, Item, and Amount fields. Our company operates on a fiscal year, but Excel doesn't provide built-in fiscal periods. We store the fiscal quarter dates and corresponding labels in a table named *tbl_qtrs*. We create a calculated field and use it to group and subtotal our PivotTable by fiscal quarter as needed.

We add the new column header, Quarter, to the data table. The formula will use the VLOOKUP function to retrieve the fiscal quarter label from the *tbl_qtrs* table. This task probably feels familiar because we've done it before.

 XREF

We used the VLOOKUP function and a fiscal quarter lookup table in Volume 2, Chapter 5.

We write the following formula to look up the transaction date and return the corresponding fiscal quarter label:

```
=VLOOKUP([@Date],tbl_qtrs,2,TRUE)
```

Where:

- **[@Date]** is the lookup value, the transaction date

- **tbl_qtrs** is the lookup range, the quarters table

- **2** is the return column

- **TRUE** means we are doing a range lookup

The table auto-fills the formula, and we easily summarize the transactions by fiscal quarter with the following report:

- PT ROWS: Quarter; VALUES: Sum(Amount)

We complete the report by formatting the value field. I like this exercise because it illustrates the concept of using a calculated field to create report groups.

EXERCISE 4—TEXT STRINGS

In this exercise, we'll split the full account code to create report groups.

 **PRACTICE**

To work along, please refer to the Exercise 4 worksheet.

The exported data is stored in the **tbl_e4_data** table on the **E4 Data** sheet and contains TransID, Date, FullAcct, and Amount columns. The full account values are comprised of a three-digit department number, a dash, and a four-digit account number, for example, 200-5030. Because we want to summarize the transactions by account and display a column for each department, we'll need to split the full account column into separate department and account columns.

We add the new column header, Dept, to the table and it auto-expands. We write the following formula to retrieve the department segment:

```
=LEFT([@FullAcct],3)
```

Where:

- **[@FullAcct]** is the full account

- **3** is the number of characters

Now that we have a department column, let's use a similar approach to create an account column. We enter the new column header, Acct, and write the following formula:

```
=RIGHT([@FullAcct],4)
```

Where:

- **[@FullAcct]** is the full account

- **4** is the number of characters

Now that we have split the full account into separate department and account columns, we easily summarize the transactions with the following report:

- PT ROWS: Acct; COLUMNS: Dept; VALUES: Sum(Amount)

We complete the report by formatting the value field.

EXERCISE 5—COMMISSION

In this exercise, we'll add a calculated field to the data table that calculates commission.

 **PRACTICE**

To work along, please refer to the Exercise 5 worksheet.

The exported sales data is stored in the *tbl_e5_data* table on the *E5 Data* sheet and contains TransID, Date, Rep, and Amount columns. Our job is to compute each rep's commission amount for payroll purposes. Previously, we faced a similar task and used a PivotTable formula to compute commission.

 XREF

We used a PivotTable formula to compute commission in Chapter 15: Calculated Fields.

In that exercise, the math was simple, and we applied the same commission rate to all representatives. In this exercise, sales reps have different rates, and we have stored them in the *tbl_rates* table. Although PivotTable restrictions prevent the formula from referencing the rates table, formulas in calculated table fields can easily retrieve these rates. We enter the new column header, Commission, into the data table and write the following formula to apply the correct commission rate to each transaction amount:

```
=[@Amount]*VLOOKUP([@Rep],tbl_rates,2,0)
```

Where:

- **[@Amount]** is the sales amount to which the commission rate is applied
- **VLOOKUP([@Rep],tbl_rates,2,0)** returns the commission rate
- **Where:**
  - ○ **[@Rep]** is the lookup value, the rep
  - ○ **tbl_rates** is the lookup range, the commission rates table
  - ○ **2** is the return column, the commission rate
  - ○ **0** for exact match

With the calculated commission field in place, we can easily summarize the transactions with the following report:

- PT ROWS: Rep; VALUES: Sum(Commission)

We complete the report by formatting the value field.

 NOTE

Another approach is to set up two calculated fields rather than one. One field retrieves the rate, and the other field computes the commission amount.

EXERCISE 6—FULL ACCOUNT

In this exercise, we'll split the full account name column into primary and subaccount columns for reporting purposes.

 **PRACTICE**

To work along, please refer to the Exercise 6 worksheet.

The exported data is stored in the ***tbl_e6_data*** table in the ***E6 Data*** sheet and contains TransID, Date, Full Account, and Amount columns. The full account values are comprised of the primary account name, a colon, and the subaccount name, for example, Marketing:Direct mail. Our report needs to provide subtotals by primary account, and within each primary account, by subaccount. Therefore we split the full account values into two columns.

We insert the first new column header, Account, into the table and use the following formula to retrieve the primary account from the full account:

```
=LEFT([@[Full Account]],FIND(":",[@[Full Account]],1)-1)
```

Where:

- **[@[Full Account]]** is the full account value
- **FIND(":",[@[Full Account]],1)-1** returns the location of the delimiter, minus one
- **Where:**
  - **":"** is the delimiter
  - **[@[Full Account]]** is the full account value
  - **1** to start searching at the first character
- **-1** subtracts one to exclude the delimiter

 NOTE

Excel automatically inserts the structured column reference [@[Full Account]] with double brackets, even though—based on previous exercises—we may have expected to see [@Full Account] with single brackets. Excel automatically surrounds the field name with additional square brackets as needed, such as when the column name includes a space.

Assuming the full account was Marketing:Direct mail, the formula evaluation sequence is:

```
=LEFT([@[Full Account]],FIND(":",[@[Full Account]],1)-1)
=LEFT([@[Full Account]],10-1)
=LEFT([@[Full Account]],9)
="Marketing"
```

We insert the next column header, Subaccount, into the table and use the following formula to retrieve the subaccount from the full account:

```
=RIGHT([@[Full Account]],LEN([@[Full Account]])-FIND(":",
[@[Full Account]],1))
```

Where:

- **[@[Full Account]]** is the full account value
- **LEN([@[Full Account]])-FIND(":",[@[Full Account]],1)** returns the number of characters
- **Where:**
  - ○ **LEN([@[Full Account]])** returns the total number of characters in the full account
  - ○ **Where:**
    - ▪ **[@[Full Account]]** is the full account value
  - ○ **FIND(":",[@[Full Account]],1)** returns the position of the delimiter
  - ○ **Where:**
    - ▪ **":"** is the delimiter
    - ▪ **[@[Full Account]]** is the full account
    - ▪ **1** to start searching at the first character

Assuming the full account value was Marketing:Direct mail, the formula evaluation sequence is:

```
=RIGHT([@[Full Account]],LEN([@[Full Account]])-FIND(":",
[@[Full Account]],1))
```

```
=RIGHT([@[Full Account]],21-FIND(":",[@[Full Account]],1))
```

```
=RIGHT([@[Full Account]],21-10)
```

```
=RIGHT([@[Full Account]],11)
```

```
="Direct mail"
```

Now that we have split the full account, we can easily build the following report:

- PT ROWS: Account, Subaccount; VALUES: Sum(Amount)

We complete the report by formatting the value field.

CHAPTER CONCLUSION

In practice we often need to prepare exported data for reporting purposes. The goal of this chapter was to explore ways to make these data transformations efficient for recurring-use workbooks.

Chapter 25: Accounting System Data

SET UP

Since accounting systems store data that is often relevant to our work, we want to optimize the process of exporting, transforming, and summarizing the data in Excel when the accounting system's built-in reports aren't sufficient for our needs. In this chapter, we apply the techniques we've discussed previously to actual extracts. Although I've used QuickBooks™ to generate the exports and illustrations in this chapter, the techniques apply broadly.

When thinking about data extracts, it is helpful to classify them as follows:

- Listing—a listing of items, such as an account list or customer list
- Transactions—a listing of transactions, such as expense transactions
- Reports—a summarized report that aggregates and groups values, such as a financial statement

Each type of extract can be useful, so let's briefly discuss them.

LISTING

A listing typically contains a list of items without transaction amounts or balances, such as a chart of accounts, customer list, or item list. We can use listings in Excel to retrieve related values, for example, to translate labels with lookup formulas.

TRANSACTIONS

Transaction extracts typically contain one row for each transaction and are often filtered for a date range or other attribute, such as account or customer. We can summarize transaction exports, including any calculated fields we may have added, with formula-based or PivotTable reports.

REPORTS

A report presents summarized data. The report can be a complex financial statement or something less elaborate, such as a trial balance. We can export canned reports to Excel when the format or layout needs to be modified for our purposes. For example, we can export a balance sheet and then pull the values into our perfectly formatted and structured formula-based report.

HOW TO

In QuickBooks you can easily export lists, transactions, and reports to Excel. For example, in QuickBooks 2014, clicking the Excel button and then selecting Create New Worksheet causes QuickBooks to display the dialog shown in Figure 72 below.

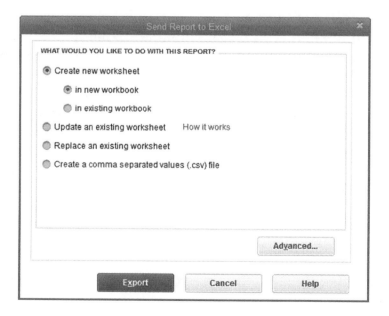

Figure 72

QuickBooks allows you to export to a new worksheet, an existing worksheet, or a CSV file. The dialog also displays an Advanced button, which offers several interesting options, such as the ability to exclude the skinny columns used as spacers. Let's briefly discuss each of the export destination options.

NEW WORKSHEET

QuickBooks can export to a new worksheet and create it in a new or existing workbook. Once the data arrives in a new sheet, we can easily copy/paste it to our recurring-use reporting workbook. Lists and transaction exports typically arrive in a flat format, while reports typically preserve their hierarchy. Do you recall our discussion about indentation? We explored three ways to indent report labels, including leading spaces, new columns, and the indent command.

 XREF

Indenting is discussed in Volume 2, Chapter 14.

QuickBooks preserves report hierarchy by indenting with new columns. Although this can present a challenge when trying to automate our workbooks, we can force reports to export in a flat format by selecting the CSV option, discussed below.

EXISTING WORKSHEET

QuickBooks can export to an existing worksheet. With this option, we save the copy/paste step required to get data from a new worksheet into our reporting workbook. We have the option to update or replace the existing sheet. If we update, QuickBooks will attempt to update the values in the worksheet while retaining custom formatting or formulas we may have added. Although we generally separate data sheets from report sheets and work with the data as it comes, it is nice to know this option exists. If we select replace, QuickBooks will replace the data on the selected sheet without attempting to retain any customizations. In either case, once QuickBooks exports updated data to the selected sheet, our reporting formulas can retrieve the values as needed.

CSV

QuickBooks can export to a new CSV file rather than to an Excel format. The benefit of this option is that reports are flat, and labels appear in a single column. Once we copy/paste the data into our reporting workbook, our report formulas can easily retrieve the values. Because Excel is best equipped to work with flat data, this is my preferred export option.

FREQUENTLY ASKED QUESTIONS

Let's explore several frequently asked questions before jumping into the exercises.

How can I eliminate the skinny spacer columns?

QuickBooks often inserts blank skinny columns between exported value columns. To exclude them from an export, open the Advanced Excel Options dialog by clicking the Advanced button shown in Figure 72 and uncheck the Space between columns checkbox.

What if the export contains more rows than last period?

Exported data may contain more rows than last period, and whenever possible we'll paste the data into a table. Otherwise we can use column-only references, such as *A:G*, in our formulas.

Can I use the external data feature?

Not directly. Excel's external data feature can retrieve data from a variety of data sources, including the CSV text files created by QuickBooks. But because Excel doesn't include built-in support for QuickBooks QBW data files, you would need to use a third-party utility or driver to gain access.

Can I customize exports?

In QuickBooks, you can customize built-in listings and reports and memorize them for future use. For example, you can add or remove columns and apply filters. It's preferable to make such customizations in the accounting system so as to minimize the amount of work required in Excel.

What about the new QuickBooks tab that appeared in the Excel Ribbon?

After installing QuickBooks, you may notice a new Ribbon tab in Excel. The Excel add-in that QuickBooks installs allows you to initiate a report refresh from within Excel.

If you want to hide the QuickBooks Ribbon tab, use the Excel Options dialog and customize the Ribbon. If you want to disable the add-in altogether, uncheck it from the COM Add-Ins dialog, which can be opened from within the Excel Options dialog as follows:

- Options > Add-ins > Manage COM Add-Ins > Go

NOTE

For more information about capabilities and limitations, please refer to the QuickBooks help system.

How do I deal with rounding issues?

It's crazy how much time accountants spend dealing with rounding issues, and it seems silly to devote so much time to chasing down a couple of cents. But that is our world. We often encounter rounding issues when the precision of displayed and stored values is different, such as when the stored value includes cents but the displayed value shows whole dollars. Excel formulas operate on stored values, not displayed values, and Excel may therefore compute a different total than a user would when summing the displayed values. Here are some ideas to consider when you experience these types of issues:

- Same precision level
- Accept displayed and stored value differences
- Excel ROUND function
- Plug

Same precision level: When displaying and storing the same level of precision is viable, for example when both the displayed and stored values include cents, life is easy. When this is not acceptable, we'll consider the next possibility.

 NOTE

Excel provides an option to permanently truncate stored values to match the precision of displayed values. Although I don't use it in practice, the Set precision as displayed option is located in the Excel Options dialog.

Accept displayed and stored value differences: Another option is to accept displayed and stored values differences. This is the approach that Intuit uses when generating QuickBooks reports. It acknowledges that a computer total based on stored values may differ from a total derived by footing the displayed values. The exercise workbook includes a screenshot of a QuickBooks report that reflects 200,096 for total current assets, even though the total is 200,095 when footed based on displayed values. When this treatment is acceptable, life is easy. When this is not acceptable, we'll consider the next possibility.

NOTE

When QuickBooks reports that are set to display without cents are exported to Excel, the values are stored as whole dollars. This report option is on the fonts and numbers tab of the Report Customization dialog box.

Excel ROUND function: When we export data to a worksheet and retrieve the values with Excel formulas, we can integrate the ROUND function to ensure the rounded values are stored and displayed in our report. The subtotal formulas will sum the rounded report values, and thus the report will foot on its face.

 XREF

The ROUND function is discussed in Volume 1, Chapter 17.

Because this approach can result in reports that aren't internally consistent, for example, total assets may not equal total liabilities and equity, you'll want to be sure to use a good error check sheet to detect potential issues.

 XREF

Error check sheets are discussed in Volume 2, Chapter 25.

Plug: Another option is to create a formula that applies the difference to a selected line item, but this technique has many drawbacks. For example, it can be difficult to maintain internal consistency between reports issued in current and future periods. Additionally this technique results in inconsistent report formulas, and, as you know, we prefer to write consistent formulas.

Why do I see the formula instead of the formula result in an exported worksheet?

If you have ever exported a report from QuickBooks and then written a formula in that worksheet, you may have noticed that the formula is displayed in the cell instead of the formula result. This is due to the way QuickBooks formats the cells. To remedy this, you can change the cell formatting to General before writing the formula. If you've already entered the formula, you can change the cell formatting and then update the formula by selecting the formula cell and then pressing F2 followed by Enter. Generally this shouldn't be an issue because our approach is to export the data and retrieve the values into separate report sheets.

 NOTE

If you need to write formulas on the exported QuickBooks sheet, please note that the CONCATENATE and TRIM functions can be handy. As described in the Excel University blog post named "Pull

Budget Values into an Income Statement," CONCATENATE can be used to combine labels that have been indented with new columns. As described in the post named "Remove Extra Spaces in Lookup Values with TRIM," the TRIM function can be used to remove padding in labels.

EXAMPLES

Won't you join me? Please open Excel and practice with several exercises.

 **PRACTICE**

To work along, please refer to *Accounting System Data.xlsx.*

 VIDEO

To watch the solutions video, please visit the Excel University Video Library.

EXERCISE 1—LIST

In this exercise, we'll need to retrieve values from an item listing exported from QuickBooks.

 **PRACTICE**

To work along, please refer to the Exercise 1 worksheet.

The exported item listing is stored on the *E1 Data* sheet and contains many columns, including Active Status, Item, Price, and Cost. We want to analyze the margin of selected products by comparing the price to the cost.

We begin by placing the selected item names on the report sheet. We create the report column headers Active Status, Price, Cost, and Margin.

Next, we'll use the powerful INDEX/MATCH combination to retrieve the status, price, and cost values from the export. We begin by populating the active status report column. We'll find the report's item label in the extract's item column and return the related status. Since the first item label is stored in *B14*, the extract's active status is stored in column *B*, and the item name is stored in column *D*, we use the following formula to populate the active status report column:

```
=INDEX('E1 Data'!B:B,MATCH(B14,'E1 Data'!D:D,0))
```

Where:

- **'E1 Data'!B:B** is the column that has the value we wish to return, the active status column

- **MATCH(B14,'E1 Data'!D:D,0)** tells the INDEX function which row has the value to return

- **Where:**

  ○ **B14** is the report label

  ○ **'E1 Data'!D:D** is the item column

  ○ **0** means exact match

We use similar formulas to populate the price and cost columns. We compute the margin by subtracting cost from price. We apply conditional formatting on the margin column, using green for values greater than zero, and red for values less than zero. To update the report for the selected items next period, we obtain an updated item list, either with a copy/paste or by exporting to this specific worksheet, and our formulas pull in the updated values.

EXERCISE 2—TRANSACTION DETAILS

In this exercise, we'll summarize exported transactions with a PivotTable.

 **PRACTICE**

To work along, please refer to the Exercise 2 worksheet.

The exported transactions are stored on the *E2 Data* sheet. Since columns *A:B* are essentially blank, we use columns *C:M* as the PivotTable data source and build the following report:

- PT ROWS: Account; VALUES: Sum(Amount); FILTERS: Type

Did you notice any unexpected behavior when building this report? When you inserted the amount field by checking its checkbox, Excel inserted it as a row field rather than a value field. This is because Excel interprets the column's data type as text rather than numeric. This also causes Excel to count, rather than sum, the field when you move it into the values area. Fortunately, we already know how to change the math to sum with the Value Field Settings dialog.

Since we are only interested in viewing paychecks, we set the type report filter to include only paychecks in the report. Since we are only interested in viewing payroll accounts in the 62700 series, we set the row field filter to show only those accounts that begin with 627. We complete the report by formatting the value field. We can easily build a PivotTable from a QuickBooks export ... no sweat.

NOTE

An alternative to using column-only references for the PivotTable data source is to copy/paste the exported data into a table. By doing this, we can exclude blank rows and avoid PivotTable issues such as grouping by date.

EXERCISE 3—REPORT

In this exercise, we'll compare retrieving values from an Excel-formatted export and a CSV-formatted export.

PRACTICE

To work along, please refer to the Exercise 3 worksheet.

We want to create a beautiful balance sheet in Excel and populate it with values retrieved from an exported QuickBooks report. We prepare the balance sheet labels and are ready to write the formulas to retrieve the values from the export. Let's compare retrieving values from the Excel-formatted export stored on the *E3 Data Excel* sheet and the CSV-formatted export stored on the *E3 Data CSV* sheet.

We begin by populating our balance sheet with the values from the Excel-formatted export stored on the *E3 Data Excel* sheet. The first balance sheet label is stored in *B13*, so we use the following formula to retrieve the value from the export:

```
=VLOOKUP(B13,'E3 Data Excel'!C:E,3,0)
```

Where:

- **B13** is the lookup value, the report label
- **'E3 Data Excel'!C:E** is the lookup range, the QuickBooks export
- **3** is the column that has the value to return, the amount column
- **0** for exact match

Looks good, but when we fill this formula down, we run into problems. For example, the formula returns an error for Fixed Assets. When we inspect the export, we notice that the report label for Fixed Assets is in column **B**, rather than column **C**. Our function can't find the label because the lookup range begins with column **C**. As we look over the entire export, we notice that QuickBooks uses columns **A:D** for labels. Since the report labels were indented using new columns rather than the indent command, the export is difficult to work with.

Let's try retrieving the values from the CSV-formatted export stored on the **E3 Data CSV** sheet. It is the same report and contains the same values. The only difference is that we exported it with the CSV option. The first balance sheet label is stored in **B13**, so we use the following formula to retrieve the value from the export:

```
=VLOOKUP(B13,'E3 Data CSV'!A:B,2,0)
```

Where:

- **B13** is the lookup value, the report label

- **'E3 Data CSV'!A:B** is the lookup range, the QuickBooks export

- **2** is the column that has the value to return, the amount column

- **0** for exact match

Looks good, and when we copy the formula down, it works for all balance sheet items! Retrieving values from the CSV export allows us to use consistent formulas and makes the workbook easy to update and maintain.

Now let me ask you a question. Would this formula work if our report labels were different from the QuickBooks labels? No, it would not. I hope you remember how to handle this situation, because you'll need to do so in the next exercise.

EXERCISE 4—TRIAL BALANCE

In this exercise, we'll use an exported trial balance to create a balance sheet, even though the labels are different.

 **PRACTICE**

To work along, please refer to the Exercise 4 worksheet.

The exported trial balance is stored on the **E4 Data** sheet. Our Excel balance sheet is stored on the **Exercise 4** worksheet and contains report labels that are different from the account labels found in the trial balance, for example Cash and Cash Equivalents instead of Checking. Fortunately, we already know how to use a map to translate the labels and aggregate several accounts, such as Checking, Savings, and Petty Cash, to a single report line, such as Cash and Cash Equivalents.

 XREF

Mapping tables are discussed in Volume 2, Chapter 23.

The mapping table is stored in the *tbl_e4_map* table on the **E4 Map** worksheet. It is similar to the previous mapping tables we've set up, with one little twist: the flip sign column. The flip sign column allows us to control the presentation of debits and credits in the balance sheet. For example, accounts payable has a credit balance but needs to flow into the balance sheet as a positive number. Let's walk through each step, as our data flows from the trial balance to the map and then to the report.

Let's start by getting the values from the trial balance to the map. To make it easy to get values from the map to the report, we'll store the amounts in a single map column. The trial balance has debit and credit columns, both of which store amounts as positive numbers. Since we want to retain information about debit and credit values, we'll pull the trial balance values into the map using simple subtraction. If we subtract the credit amount from the debit amount, positive values represent debits, and negative values represent credits. We use the following formula in our map to retrieve the trial balance amounts:

```
=SUMIFS('E4 Data'!C:C, 'E4 Data'!B:B, [@Account])-
SUMIFS('E4 Data'!D:D, 'E4 Data'!B:B, [@Account])
```

Where:

- **SUMIFS('E4 Data'!C:C,'E4 Data'!B:B,[@Account])** returns the debit amount
- **Where:**
    ○ **'E4 Data'!C:C** is the column of numbers to add, the trial balance debit column
    ○ **'E4 Data'!B:B** is the criteria range, the trial balance account column
    ○ **[@Account]** is the criteria value, the account
- **-SUMIFS('E4 Data'!D:D,'E4 Data'!B:B,[@Account])** subtracts the credit amount
- **Where:**
    ○ **'E4 Data'!D:D** is the column of numbers to add, the trial balance credit column

○ **'E4 Data'!B:B** is the criteria range, the trial balance account column

○ **[@Account]** is the criteria value, the account

This formula presents debit balances as positive numbers, and credit balances as negative numbers.

Now let's analyze the flip sign column, which gives us the ability to control how each account flows into the balance sheet. Although all debit amounts are presented as positive numbers, and all credit amounts are presented as negative numbers, we can't simply change all negative values to positive. For example, we can't change accumulated depreciation from a negative number to a positive number because then it would be added to, instead of subtracted from, the asset balance. The flip sign column provides the account-level control needed. We set the flip sign values to TRUE or FALSE as needed. Storing them as Boolean values will make our formulas easier.

 XREF

Boolean values are discussed in Volume 2, Chapter 25.

Except for depreciation data, asset accounts appear in the map as positive numbers. Because we don't need to flip their sign when they make their way to the balance sheet, we set their flip sign values to FALSE. Because liability and equity accounts appear as negative numbers in the map, we need to flip their sign for balance sheet presentation purposes and set their values to TRUE. Income accounts appear as negative amounts but need to be added to the balance sheet's equity line, so we flip their signs. Expense accounts appear as positive values but need to be subtracted from the equity line, so we flip their signs as well.

Now that the flip sign values are properly assigned, we need to modify our amount formula to flip the sign as needed. One simple way to accomplish this is by multiplying the result by −1 when the flip sign value is TRUE, and by 1 when the flip sign value is FALSE. The following conceptual formula illustrates the logic:

```
=(SUMIFS(debit)-SUMIFS(credit))*IF(FlipSign,-1,1)
```

For the final formula, we enclose the two SUMIFS functions in parentheses to control the order of operation, and tack on an IF function, as follows:

```
=(SUMIFS('E4 Data'!C:C,'E4 Data'!B:B,[@Account])-
SUMIFS('E4 Data'!D:D,'E4 Data'!B:B,[@Account]))
*IF([@FlipSign],-1,1)
```

Where:

- **SUMIFS('E4 Data'!C:C,'E4 Data'!B:B,[@Account])** returns the debit amount

- **-SUMIFS('E4 Data'!D:D,'E4 Data'!B:B,[@Account])** returns the credit amount

- ***IF([@FlipSign],-1,1)** flips the sign as needed

- **Where:**

  - **[@FlipSign]** considers the value in the flip sign column

  - **-1** if flip sign is TRUE, multiply the amount by minus one

  - **1** if flip sign is FALSE, multiply the amount by one

The map's amount column now includes values ready for the balance sheet.

Since we carefully prepared the map, we can use a consistent formula to populate the entire balance sheet report. The first report label is stored in *B12*, and we write the following formula to populate the first report line:

```
=SUMIFS(tbl_e4_map[Amount],tbl_e4_map[FSLine],B12)
```

Where:

- **tbl_e4_map[Amount]** is the column of numbers to add, the amount column

- **tbl_e4_map[FSLine]** is the criteria range, the report label column

- **B12** is the criteria value, the report label

We copy the formula down to all balance sheet rows and smile. We can update the report in future periods by exporting a new trial balance from QuickBooks and getting it into the data sheet. The map automatically retrieves the values, and the balance sheet amounts are updated accordingly.

CHAPTER CONCLUSION

I hope that the techniques demonstrated in this chapter will come in handy and help automate the flow of data from your accounting system to your Excel reports.

Chapter 26: Getting Graphic

SET UP

In this chapter, we'll put a pretty little bow on our reporting packages. The formula-based and PivotTable reports we've created thus far have been presented in a table format that contains rows and columns of numbers. We can also present data graphically. Tables and graphs each have benefits, and selecting the right format for a particular report depends on the audience, data, and message. When your message requires precision, a table is a great choice. When your message conveys trends or relationships, consider a graph. Fortunately, Excel offers numerous ways to get graphic.

In this chapter, we'll explore several Excel features that provide the ability to communicate information graphically, including PivotCharts, traditional charts, conditional formatting, and sparklines. This chapter covers the features at an introductory level and essentially provides a getting started guide. If a specific feature looks like it will be a good fit for your workbooks, feel free to take a deeper dive and explore the details. Excel's graphics capabilities are impressive, and there are entire books dedicated to charts, graphs, and dashboards.

HOW TO

Let's talk through each of the following features:

- PivotChart

- Traditional chart

- Conditional formatting

- Sparkline

We've dedicated much of our time this volume to PivotTables, and I hope that you love them. If you do, then I'm sure you'll also love PivotCharts.

PIVOTCHART

The PivotChart feature is useful when your worksheet contains transaction details rather than summary balances. A PivotTable summarizes transaction details. A PivotChart plots the values of a specific PivotTable. The PivotChart and PivotTable are linked, and changes made to one impact the other. For example, if you group a PivotTable by month, the related PivotChart will reflect months. If you group a PivotChart by quarter, the related PivotTable will reflect quarters. A PivotChart simply displays the values presented in a PivotTable.

To create a PivotChart from an existing PivotTable, activate the PivotTable and select the following Ribbon command:

- PivotTable Tools > Analyze > PivotChart

You'll be able to select from a variety of chart types, such as line, column, or pie. You'll want to be sure to select the most appropriate chart type. For example, column and bar charts are a great way to display values across categories, such as sales by region. Line charts are a great way to present trends over time, such as monthly sales. Pie charts are a great way to show percentages of a whole, such as the contribution of each item to total sales. Excel provides numerous chart types and design options, and you'll want to fully explore the following PivotChart Tools Ribbon tabs:

- Analyze—analyze the data with filters and calculations

- Design—design the chart with style options and chart types

- Format—format chart elements with various settings and shapes

By default Excel creates new charts as floating objects in the drawing layer of a worksheet. You are free to move charts around the worksheet, and resize them as needed. You can place several charts on a worksheet if you need to deliver them in a single PDF or printed page. You can also move the chart from the drawing layer to a chart sheet. A chart sheet is like a worksheet that only contains a chart. A chart sheet is represented by a tab next to the other worksheets. To move the chart, select the following Ribbon icon:

- PivotChart Tools > Design > Move Chart

The PivotChart feature is a great fit when you need to prepare a graph from transaction details. But if your worksheet already has summary values, consider using a traditional chart.

TRADITIONAL CHART

Creating a chart from summary values is fairly easy with the traditional charting feature. You can create a chart from an ordinary range or a table. If your chart data is stored in a table, you'll easily be able to add new rows in future periods and apply table filters that carry through to the chart.

To insert a traditional chart into your worksheet, simply select a cell in the range and then the desired chart type button from the following Ribbon group:

- Insert > Charts

The capabilities, options, and design alternatives are similar to PivotCharts, and you'll want to be sure to explore the following Chart Tools Ribbon tabs:

- Design—design the chart with style options and chart types
- Format—format chart elements with various settings and shapes

Since charts exclude hidden columns and rows, you can centrally store all chart data on a single sheet and hide columns as needed. When you hide a column on your chart data sheet, all charts in the workbook are instantly updated. If the chart data is not centrally located and instead is placed on numerous sheets, you'll have to hide columns on many sheets. For example, if you store the chart data on a single sheet and hide the December column, then all charts will exclude December. This technique makes is easy to maintain recurring-use workbooks that contain several time-based charts, since you only need to hide columns on one data sheet, rather than many.

If a PivotChart or a traditional chart is just too big and fancy, and all you need is something simple, consider adding a graphic element to your reports with the conditional formatting feature.

CONDITIONAL FORMATTING

Conditional formatting supports icon sets and data bars and can add a graphical element to your reporting workbook when space is limited or when you just want to create something fast and easy. Conditional formatting automatically updates when the data is updated, making it a beautiful option for recurring-use workbooks. Because we've already covered the mechanics for this feature, we'll move along.

 XREF

Conditional formatting is discussed in Volume 1, Chapter 10.

If you have limited space and want to create a tiny little chart, consider using a sparkline.

SPARKLINE

A sparkline is a chart that occupies a single worksheet cell. Since it uses such a small space, it lacks the precision and detail offered by traditional charts and PivotCharts, but when space is limited, this is a great way to add visual information to your reports.

To insert a sparkline, select the destination range and then click the icon for the desired type from the following Ribbon group:

- Insert > Sparklines

The resulting Create Sparklines dialog box contains two range input fields, one for the data range, and the other for the sparkline location.

Figure 73 below illustrates line and column sparklines.

	B	C	D	E	F	G	H
10		Month				Sparkline	
11	Region	Jan	Feb	Mar		Line	Column
12	North	10,158	12,228	13,557			
13	South	11,005	8,690	10,722			
14	East	12,052	10,963	13,790			
15	West	9,050	12,681	14,662			

Figure 73

Once the sparkline is set up, you have a variety of design and style options to explore. Take your time and work through the icons on the following Ribbon tab:

- Sparkline Tools > Design

These four features, PivotCharts, traditional charts, conditional formatting, and sparklines, allow us to visually communicate our message to our report users.

FREQUENTLY ASKED QUESTIONS

Let's explore several frequently asked questions before jumping into the exercises.

How can I get my chart into another program?

There are several ways to get an Excel chart into another application. Some applications support static images, while others may also support dynamic links to the Excel source file. One way to create a static image from an Excel chart is to copy the chart, flip to another worksheet, and select the Paste Picture icon. The resulting picture can now be cut or copied and pasted into other applications. Another way is to use the Windows snipping utility. This utility is convenient because it provides an option to save the image to a file as well as copy it to the clipboard. Additionally, you can copy the chart and flip to the destination application to explore various paste options. Some applications may insert a static image, while others, such as Word® and PowerPoint®, may offer the option to paste a linked chart, which updates when the Excel chart is updated. Please explore the help system of the destination application as needed.

What are SmartArt Graphics?

SmartArt Graphics offer a variety of visually impactful ways to communicate your message. For example, they can help represent lists, process flows, hierarchy, and relationships. You can insert a SmartArt Graphic with the following Ribbon icon:

- Insert > SmartArt Graphics

This will open the Choose a SmartArt Graphic dialog box shown in Figure 74 below.

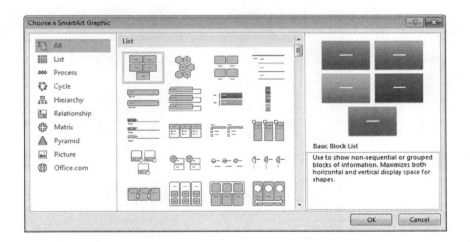

Figure 74

Browse through to select the most appropriate type for the information you are communicating. The selected graphic is inserted into your worksheet. There are many stunning design options that you can play with on the following SmartArt Tools Ribbon tabs:

- Design—design the graphic with layouts and styles
- Format—format the graphic with fills and shape options

The SmartArt Graphics feature will make you look like a graphic design rock star.

Can I insert a shape or a picture?

Yes. If you need to insert a simple shape, such as an arrow or box, check out the following Ribbon icon:

- Insert > Shapes

There are numerous design options available on the related Ribbon tab:

- Drawing Tools > Format

If you want to insert an image from your computer, such as a picture, check out the following Ribbon icon:

- Insert > Pictures

There are numerous formatting commands available on the related Ribbon tab:

- Picture Tools > Format

If you want to insert an image from Microsoft's royalty-free clip art gallery, check out the following Ribbon icon:

- Insert > Online Pictures

There are numerous formatting commands available on the related Ribbon tab:

- Picture Tools > Format

These images are inserted into the drawing layer of the worksheet and can be resized and positioned as needed.

What is the REPT function?

The REPT function is a worksheet function that repeats a character a certain number of times. It can be used to simulate bar charts in very basic applications. The function's syntax follows:

```
=REPT(text,number_times)
```

Where:

- **text** is the text string or character to repeat

- **number_times** is the number of times to repeat it, expressed as a number, cell reference, function, or expression

To simulate a bar chart, you can have Excel repeat a character, such as an equal sign, a specific number of times, as illustrated in Figure 75 below.

	B	C	D
14	**Rep**	**Quantity**	**REPT**
15	DAR	10	==========
16	JUB	7	=======
17	DMK	3	===
18	GSL	5	=====
19	BYG	12	============
20	BEO	8	========

Figure 75

You can format the REPT formula cells with graphic fonts, such as Webdings or Wingdings, to create interesting and fun graphics. If you want to quickly view the characters for any given font, simply use the Windows Character Map utility or the following Ribbon icon:

- Insert > Symbol

What is an easy way to make my formatting look good?

Probably the easiest way to format a worksheet is by using the cell styles available in the following Ribbon icon:

- Home > Cell Styles

How can I pull a cell value into a text box?

If you'd like to pull a cell value into a text box located in the worksheet or in a chart, select the text box, enter an equal sign in the formula bar, select the cell, and hit Enter. Because text box formulas are limited to retrieving a cell value, you'll need to perform any necessary calculations with the cell's formula, for example, combining text strings and values with the CONCATENATE function.

EXAMPLES

It is time to crack open the final exercise workbook of the volume and build a few PivotCharts.

 **PRACTICE**

To work along, please refer to *Getting Graphic.xlsx*.

 VIDEO

To watch the solutions video, please visit the Excel University Video Library.

EXERCISE 1—COLUMN CHART

In this exercise, we'll create a column PivotChart.

 **PRACTICE**

To work along, please refer to the Exercise 1 worksheet.

The exported sales data is stored in the *tbl_data* table on the *Data* sheet and contains TransID, Region, Rep, Item, Date, and Amount columns. We want to summarize the transactions by region and present the report graphically to make it easy to visualize the relative performance of each region. We decide to use a column chart to display the values across regions.

Since we have transaction details and not summary values, we'll create a PivotTable to summarize the data and a PivotChart to present it. We begin by creating the following report:

* PT ROWS: Region; VALUES: Sum(Amount)

Now for the PivotChart. We activate the PivotTable and select the following Ribbon command:

* PivotTable Tools > Analyze > PivotChart

In the resulting Insert Chart dialog box, we select the desired column chart format and click OK. Bam, Excel drops the PivotChart into our worksheet. Wow ... we went from transaction detail to a chart in about a minute!

EXERCISE 2—LINE CHART

In this exercise, we'll create a line PivotChart.

 **PRACTICE**

To work along, please refer to the Exercise 2 worksheet.

Using the data from the previous exercise, we want to view the sales trend over time. This sounds like a perfect fit for a line chart. The first step is to summarize the transactions with the following PivotTable report:

- PT ROWS: Month(Date); VALUES: Sum(Amount)

We activate the PivotTable and insert a line PivotChart. Hey, that was fast!

EXERCISE 3—PIE CHART

In this exercise, we'll build a pie PivotChart.

 **PRACTICE**

To work along, please refer to the Exercise 3 worksheet.

Using the data from the previous exercise, we want to view each item's relative contribution to total sales. Since we want to see the parts of a whole, this sounds like a job for a pie chart. We begin by building the following PivotTable:

- PT ROWS: Item; VALUES: Sum(Amount)

We activate the PivotTable and insert a pie PivotChart. Looks good, but the chart displays the items in alphabetical order rather than in sales order. We can make the chart look better by sorting the PivotTable descending by amount. Ah, yes, that looks better.

EXERCISE 4—EXTERNAL DATA

In this exercise, we'll build a PivotChart to graphically analyze and display familiar data stored in an external data source.

 **PRACTICE**

To work along, please refer to the Exercise 4 worksheet.

This will be the fourth time we've used this data. At the end of Volume 2, we stored the data in an Excel worksheet and created a formula-based report to summarize it. Next, we stored the same data in a worksheet and used a PivotTable to summarize it. Then we stored it in an Access database and summarized it with a PivotTable. Now the data is stored in an Access database, and we'll present it graphically with a PivotChart. Excited? (Me too!)

Here's the scenario. On a monthly basis we present each department's SG&A expenses in a column chart. Our current process takes about an hour. We open our accounting system and export the data to a file. We open the file and copy and paste the data into an Excel worksheet. We spend time formatting and preparing the data for use. We manually summarize the transactions by department and then create a column chart.

Let's see if we can reduce the time it takes to complete this process. Let's use the external data feature to retrieve the data, a PivotTable to summarize it, and a PivotChart to display it.

The data is stored in the ***tbl_transactions*** table in the ***AccessDB.accdb*** database. First we need to retrieve the data. We launch the Query Wizard and walk through the steps to identify the table, all columns, and all rows. In the resulting Import Data dialog box, we elect to send the data directly into a PivotTable. We create the following report:

- PT ROWS: Dept; VALUES: Sum(Amount)

We activate the PivotTable and insert a column PivotChart. Wow … this is beautiful! To update the chart next period, all we'll need to do is refresh the PivotTable. Transactions automatically flow from the database into the PivotTable and PivotChart. We could easily add month or quarter filters to the PivotTable if needed. The manual process that used to take about an hour is now complete with a single click. Dude, I love Excel!

CHAPTER CONCLUSION

This chapter highlights several of Excel's many options for presenting information graphically. Please continue to explore the ones most relevant to your work.

Conclusion

My primary goal for this volume is to provide you with a solid working knowledge of PivotTables. The first section served as a warm-up to discuss the basics and show how to recreate Volume 2's final formula-based report with a PivotTable.

The second section demonstrated many design and layout options needed to replace formula-based reports with PivotTables, and we recreated numerous formula-based reports with PivotTables.

The third section discussed strategies for optimizing more of the Excel reporting process, including getting data into our workbooks, transforming and preparing that data, and then summarizing and displaying it.

I hope that the topics presented help to improve your productivity. And remember, Excel rules!

Shortcut Reference

The following list reflects the shortcuts presented through this volume

Shortcut	Action	Volume	Chapter
Arrow Keys	Navigate within worksheet and cell values	1	6
Shift+Arrow Keys	Extend selection	1	6
Ctrl+Arrow Keys	Jump to edge of region or word	1	6
Ctrl+A	Select all cells in region	1	6
F2	Edit mode	1	6
F4	Cycles through cell reference styles (absolute, relative, mixed)	1	6
Double-click fill handle	Fill formula down	1	6
Ctrl+PageUp/ PageDown	Activate previous/next sheet	1	6
Alt+=	Insert SUM function	1	6
F5	GoTo	1	7
Ctrl+T and Alt+N,T	Insert table	1	8
Alt+N,T	Insert table	1	8
Alt+D, L	Data validation	1	9
Alt+A,V,V	Data validation	1	9
Alt+Down Arrow	Expand drop-down	1	9
F3	Paste name	1	9

Alt+I, N, D	Insert name	1	9
Alt+M, N	Insert name	1	9
Ctrl+F3	Insert name	1	9
Alt+O, R, E	Format row height	1	12
Alt+I, R	Insert row	1	12
Alt+H, I, R	Insert row	1	12
Alt+O, C, W	Format column width	1	12
Alt+O, H, H	Hide sheet	1	13
Alt+O, H, U	Unhide sheet	1	13
Alt+O, H, R	Rename sheet	1	15
Alt+E, L	Delete active sheet	1	15
Alt+I, W	Insert worksheet	1	15
Ctrl+Enter	Enter formula and fill it down	1	18
Shift+Ctrl+PageUp/ PageDown	Group select adjacent sheets	1	18
F9	Convert formula text to evaluated result	2	2
Alt+E, I, D	Fill down	2	2
Ctrl+D	Fill down	2	2
Alt+E, I, R	Fill right	2	2
Ctrl+R	Fill right	2	2
Ctrl+C	Copy	2	2
Ctrl+V	Paste	2	2
Alt+E, S	Paste special	2	2
Ctrl+Alt+V	Paste special	2	2
Ctrl+Home	Jump to A1	2	2
Shift+Space	Select entire row	2	2
Alt+E, D	Delete selected row or column	2	2
Ctrl+-	Delete selected row or column	2	2
Alt+I, C	Insert column	2	2
Alt+H, I, C	Insert column	2	2
Ctrl+Space	Select entire column	2	2
Ctrl+Shift+Space	Select all cells	2	2
Alt+O, R, E	Format row height	2	2
Alt+H, 6	Increase indent	2	14
Alt+H, 5	Decrease indent	2	14

Alt+O, D	Conditional Formatting	2	25
Ctrl+PageUp/ PageDown	Dialog box tab control navigation	3	2
Alt+Underlined Letter	Activate dialog box control with underlined letter	3	2
Tab	Navigate through dialog box controls and fields	3	2
Shift+Tab	Navigate through dialog box controls in reverse order	3	2
Arrows	Select values in certain dialog controls such as a combo box	3	2
Letters	Jump to items within certain dialog box controls such as list boxes	3	2
Space	Toggle selection in certain dialog box controls such as a check box	3	2
Enter	Activate OK button in dialog box to accept changes	3	2
Esc	Activate Cancel button to close dialog without saving changes	3	2
Ctrl+1	Open Format Cells dialog box	3	2
Alt+O, E	Open Format Cells dialog box	3	2
Alt+D, R	Refresh PivotTable data while active	3	8
Alt+D, P	Legacy PivotTable Wizard	3	8

Index

75946559R00165

Made in the USA
Columbia, SC
28 August 2017